Every time I read Melinda Means, I feel like I've encountered the heart of Christ. In *Invisible Wounds*, she goes one step further. She shows me how Christ is holding my heart in his hands, and how He holds me gently—every wound, every broken place—to bring wholeheartedness to my life. This book is for any woman who is hurting today, any woman who needs to know that hope is one heart-cry away.

~ **Jennifer Dukes Lee**,
author of *Love Idol* and *The Happiness Dare*

In *Invisible Wounds*, Melinda gets real and encourages us to do the same. It's through this realness that we can find grace from God and stronger relationships with others. Stories from Melinda's life, her friends' stories, and examples from Scripture all work together to help readers view their hardships as the training ground for growth. I'm excited to have this book to recommend to the special-needs parents that I minister to each day.

~ **Sandra Peoples**,
author of *Held: Learning to Live in God's Grip* (a Bible Study for Special-Needs Parents) and site editor for Key Ministry, *keyministry.org*

Melinda shares her battle to find hope and hold onto her faith as she copes with the challenges of her personal debilitating disease, as well as the condition of her precious son. She allows you to see and feel her struggles and numbness all while being transparent about her doubts and questions about God. Her book will bring much-needed inspiration to others who have invisible wounds, too.

~ **Amy Lykins**,
Executive Director of Business Development at
Proverbs 31 Ministries, *proverbs31.org*

This is the perfect book for anyone fighting a battle that might not be obvious to those around them. Whether dealing with physical pain no one can see or emotional wounds that haunt your prayers, this book will remind you you're not alone, and there's power in sharing your story. Your wounds might be invisible to others, but they aren't invisible to God. He sees. And He cares. This book makes that abundantly clear.

~ **Lindsey Bell**,
author of *Unbeaten:
How Biblical heroes rose above their pain…and you can, too.*
and *Searching for Sanity: 52 Insights from Parents of the Bible*

It's rare to find someone who will share her wounds with the kind of vulnerability Melinda does… Her voice is powerful yet tender. She will challenge you and encourage you at the same time. And chances are, you'll laugh and cry…and maybe even find yourself nodding with a deep understanding as you read the hard-earned wisdom in these pages.

~ **Carey Scott**,
author of *Untangled: Let God Loosen the
Knots of Insecurity in Your Life*

Foreword

I met Melinda many years ago and felt an instant connection with her. There are times you meet someone extra special and bypass the shallows for the deeper waters. It's not forced. It's not awkward. Instead it feels right because you recognize a kindred spirit. That was my experience with Melinda.

I've been writing and speaking for twelve years now. My greatest desire is to see women freed from the insecurities tangling their self-worth and knotting them up in worthlessness, shame, fear and unforgiveness. My most recent book, *Untangled: Let God Loosen the Knots of Insecurity in Your Life*, is an anthem for honesty and healing. I'm a crusader in the battle of authenticity, and I want women to know they are already loved, accepted and deeply valuable to the One who created them...no matter what. Because this topic is so close to my heart, I am genuinely honored to be a part of *Invisible Wounds*.

What I appreciate about Melinda the most is her willingness to talk about the tough stuff—the exhausting struggles and offenses many of us keep tucked away. Sometimes it's easier to put on a brave face rather than open our lives for others to see. It's rare to find someone who will share her wounds with the kind of vulnerability Melinda does. But it's in her honesty you'll find comfort and camaraderie in knowing you're not alone.

This is the kind of book we need right now because trying to look like we have it all together is absolutely wearing us out. When did we start buying into the lie that says our struggles are weaknesses? Why won't we let others see what's really going on inside? Why are we stuffing our pain instead of asking for help? And why are we angry with God for not doing what we want, when we want?

Well buckle up, friend, because this book asks the hard questions that have felt too overwhelming to ask for ourselves—much less try to answer. Melinda honestly shares her journey of grappling with God and the insights she's received in the midst of it. If you're questioning God's goodness…if you're wondering why He allows suffering…if you can't understand why He doesn't save us from pain…you're in for a good read. Over and over again, I shook my head and smiled because Melinda's boldness is terribly refreshing. It's about time we enter into an honest conversation about what we're really thinking and feeling, and being truthful about the battles we're fighting.

In its pages, Melinda introduces you to seven women who—aside from herself—bravely share their invisible wounds. I was so moved by their transparency. The truth is, their stories mirror my story. You may see *your* story in these pages. These women paint a powerful picture of what it looks like when God intersects with our pain. You will appreciate the raw honesty in each chapter and find comfort in knowing you're not forgotten. Because you're not. *God sees you.* He always has.

I know firsthand the burden of carrying invisible wounds. From sexual abuse at age four to intense feelings of worthlessness to painful words from others to guilt in parenting to agonizing seasons in marriage, I've carried so much pain alone—buried and unseen. Maybe it's because I didn't want to be judged or criticized. Maybe I was afraid the negative narrative about me would end up being the truth. Maybe I believed no one really cared. Regardless of why I let those wounds fester, this book gave me permission to exhale the lies and breathe in truth.

Chances are you have invisible wounds, too. They might be the result of unmanageable addictions, incredible loss, serious health issues, deep disappointments, heavy shame, embarrassing choices, abuse of all kinds or from a myriad of other struggles. And because it feels too risky to be real, you've learned to stuff and smile. The wounds may be hemorrhaging inside, but no one would ever know it. Sweet one, this is *not* how God created you to respond to life. Let's learn to live differently.

You will love the candor of my friend, Melinda. She just has a way with words. Her voice is powerful yet tender. She will challenge you and encourage you at the same time.

Invisible Wounds

And chances are, you'll laugh and cry...and maybe even find yourself nodding with a deep understanding as you read the hard-earned wisdom in these pages.

I'm proud of you for holding this book in your hands. And I promise that if you let Him, God will meet you in it and heal those invisible wounds from the inside out.

~ **Carey Scott**
CareyScottTalks.com, Author,
Untangled: Let God Loosen the Knots of Insecurity in Your Life
and *Uncommon: Pursuing a Life of Passion and Purpose*
(release date, July 1, 2017)

Tears are words that need to be written.
~ Pablo Coehlo

Dear Hurting Woman,

Writing this book has been a part of my healing. I pray that as you read it God will use it to be part of yours, as well. As I wrote, at times I fought overwhelming discouragement. During one of those times, a good friend told me, "Think about the hurting woman out there who needs your words. Write to *her*."

So, I did. I wrote to *you*. I'm not sure how. I honestly look back and marvel at how God weaved my scattered thoughts and words together, especially during those times of pain and discouragement.

This book doesn't just tell *my* story. Seven brave, beautiful women also share their invisible wounds in these pages. Most are using assumed names due to the sensitive nature of their wounds and/or because of how it might affect others who are associated with their stories. Sharing their pain for this book often brought them to tears. Yet, each one gladly went to some very dark, vulnerable places. They believed God wanted to use their heartache to relieve someone else's. I am so grateful for these amazing ladies. God is going to use their obedience to bring hope and healing.

Does your pain feel invisible, friend? God sees you. Every wound. Every tear. He is the Hope who heals.

Love, Melinda

CHAPTER 1

The Pain That No One Sees

You look at me and think, *she's so happy*, but there's so much behind this little smile that you will never know.

~ Unknown

Every time I look in the mirror, I see it.

Fear, pain, brokenness, doubts, disillusionment, and discouragement all stare back at me. They've been a part of how I see myself for so long that I honestly can't remember what I looked like before. At times, they seem to envelop and define me.

When the world looks at me, they see someone very different.

They see a bright, warm smile, a tall, impossibly thin frame, a cute bob hairstyle and fashionable clothes—a confident, put-together woman.

Many days, however, I'm teetering on the verge of falling apart—physically, emotionally and spiritually. My cool exterior masks my daily pain. Every morning, I wake up and put on a smile.

1

Invisible Wounds

No one can see my invisible wounds.

I think back to one of my favorite photos* of my children. Molly was three. Micah was nine months old. They look absolutely enchantingly adorable. Everyone's smiling and looks happy. It's just the perfect photo—no easy feat with little ones. But let me share the story behind this "perfect" snapshot.

I had done all the right things to prepare for the child photography experience. They both had a nap, they'd been fed, and they were dressed in the required darling matching outfits. I was golden.

We arrived at the mall. That's when it got interesting. I lifted my son Micah from his car seat just as he had a diaper blowout of legendary proportions. I used every baby wipe I had and he was still a poopy mess. I was so close to photo-taking victory I could smell it (unfortunately that's not *all* I could smell).

So I wrapped him in a blanket and with my daughter in tow we high tailed it through the mall parking lot to find the nearest bathroom. On the way, my daughter tripped and fell, ripping a hole in her white tights and scraping her knee. Time to throw in the towel? Nope. This newest setback only made me more determined.

In the bathroom, we made the tragic discovery: hand dryers—no paper towels. As my daughter handed me reams of toilet paper, I went to work cleaning up my son. We finally made it to the photo studio. The result? *Adorable*. My son's plaid outfit masked the stains (if not the smell). My daughter's strategically placed little hand covered that wound on her knee. No one would ever guess the trauma that had gone on behind the scenes.

Looks can be deceiving, can't they? Our pain lurks beneath the surface, camouflaged by busyness, a confident demeanor, or a tough outer shell. Maybe you're grieving the loss of a marriage or a child. Perhaps you're carrying wounds from sexual abuse, a heartbreaking childhood, a prodigal child, or a broken or difficult relationship.

We hide because we think no one else will understand. Maybe we think we're to blame. We're afraid of rejection. We believe it makes us weak. We don't want others to feel sorry for us. We don't want our pain to define us.

So we nurse our pain in isolation. We live alone with our invisible wounds.

Like so many of us, my wounds are numerous. Some are too private to share with the world. Some involve other people. I can't share those wounds publicly right now without wounding someone else. Genuine, lasting healing will never come by inflicting pain on another. One day the time might be right for me to share these hidden hurts, but not now. Most of the women sharing their stories in this book are using assumed names. They are doing so primarily for these reasons.

The wounds I believe God wants me to expose in this book stem from the trauma that began on what should have been one of the most joyful days of my life—the day my first child was born. My labor and delivery had been an incredibly difficult ordeal. Within twenty-four hours, I felt extreme bladder pain and urgency. Although I tested negative for infection, the doctor prescribed antibiotics. By the end of the week, my antibiotics were gone, but my pain was not. I went to the doctor multiple times over the next few weeks. I was passed from doctor to doctor, but never received any solutions.

Invisible Wounds

When I left the urologist's care in search of answers elsewhere, I asked for my records. In his notes the doctor wrote, "Twenty-seven-year-old female comes to the office without appointment, complaining of active, ongoing bladder pain. However, nurse reports that she doesn't appear in distress and seems to be enjoying her new baby."

> My hope doesn't depend on my healing, but my Healer.

I didn't look sick. I didn't appear to be in pain. Day by day, I managed to hold it together for my baby and my husband.

For a time I quit going to doctors and turned to Google instead. After many desperate searches, I discovered my pain had a name: interstitial cystitis. It's an inflammatory, autoimmune disease and it usually has "friends." Over the years, I have developed migraines, joint and muscle pain, chronic fatigue, lower back pain, hypothyroidism, and anemia. In essence, my body is attacking itself. Although I've had periods of remission, the pain always comes back. Over the past seven years, my days without pain have been rare.

At the same time, I have a son who is waging his own invisible battle. He looks fine, yet he fights for every breath. Every day cystic fibrosis tries to steal it from him—along with his carefree childhood and his joy. Like mine, it's a wound that won't heal emotionally or physically. As his mother, I carry his wound, too. Seeing my child suffer has been, in some ways, a wound deeper than my own.

Years of disappointment, isolation and discouragement

have scarred me. Because I never know how I'm going to feel, I struggle to make plans or fully engage in life. I feel the weight of my son's pain. My anxiety and insecurity—always a struggle—has sometimes felt nearly unbearable. At times, it has shaken my faith to its very core.

The High Cost of Hidden Pain

Regardless of its source, our disappointment, pain, and disillusionment can cause us to question a good and loving God. We struggle to understand why He has left us in our pain. We become disillusioned when we consider that an all-powerful God refuses to grant us healing from our wounds.

I don't think God is afraid of our desperate questioning. In Psalms, David pours out his heart and feelings of abandonment to God. His raw emotions and frustrations are a running theme throughout his writings. At times, in pure exhaustion and disappointment, my tear-soaked rants have simply given way to silence.

Questioning and silence both have their place at times. But we have to be careful not to stay in either place too long. That is when we lose perspective. We begin to believe the lies. We put up an emotional barrier in our relationship with God to protect ourselves from disappointment.

Isolation is one of Satan's favorite and most effective weapons. We need people around us to give us perspective, and reassure us that God is listening and active in our situations, even when we can't see or feel Him. Often, though, our tendency is to withdraw and suffer in silence. When we're alone in our pain, we can easily convince ourselves that we are the only one struggling like this. No one cares about our pain. Some of us live in shame, believing people would judge us or blame us for our problems. It leaves us incredibly vulnerable to discouragement, despair, and hopelessness. The lies we believe about God take root.

I understand. For years, I told virtually no one about my health struggles. I downplayed their impact on my life. *Others have it so much worse*, I would tell myself. Maybe I'm just weak and can't hack it. Nobody wants to hear about my problems. I was ashamed. I thought no one would understand. I didn't want it to define me.

But over the last year, through a series of painful events, God brought me to my knees. Out of desperation and necessity, I began to reach out. For the first time, I publicly told my story of pain and wrestling with God. The response was staggering. I literally felt like a huge burden was lifted from me, even though my circumstance had not changed. We were meant for community, friend. It is what will kick start your healing.

Searching for the Healer

So what do we do with our pain? Where is God in all this? Why does a loving, compassionate God allow us to suffer in this way? How do we find peace and joy in circumstances and pain that may never go away? How do we cope with feeling alone with our hidden wounds? Here's the truth: I don't have all the answers. Frankly, it scares me to write this book. I have a finite view of God's ways. Others have suffered with wounds far deeper and more painful than mine. But I feel compelled to tell my story.

Humanly, here's the book I wish I could write: "I went through this terrible time and I'm on the other side now and here are three easy steps for how you can overcome, too." Unfortunately, there is no quick one-size-fits-all formula for rising above our pain. My journey has been long and messy with a lot fewer answers. The truth is that I'm still right in the middle of this painful battle. I'm not sure when I'm going to see the other side of it. Sometimes, quite frankly, I don't feel God in the middle of it.

I don't have all the answers. But here's something important that I *do* know: God is not afraid of our questions. He isn't surprised or appalled by our frustrated, tear-soaked temper tantrums (I've had more than a few). He just wants us to come to Him.

For years, I have looked for an outcome. Relief from my pain. I wanted healing. Period. I still do. But I've learned healing can look very different than what we imagine. Hope and healing can come through telling our stories. It can materialize as God meets us and reveals Himself in the middle of our struggle. It can materialize as we see God redeem our pain.

This isn't the path I would have chosen for myself. It isn't the journey I would have chosen for my son. Yet pain leads us to a deeper walk with God if we are open to gifts that we would never have received without our pain. Others receive gifts they wouldn't have received without our pain.

God cares. He sees your struggle, sweet friend. But He wants to do so much more than change our pain. He wants to use our pain to change *us*. When our joy, freedom, and hope rest on an outcome, instead of a Person, we will ultimately be disappointed. Our circumstances are just too shaky and unpredictable. God never changes. We are always on solid ground when He is the Source of our hope. It is not through the *result*—the relief of our emotional, physical, or spiritual suffering—that the most important transformation comes. It is through the *relationship* with Jesus.

I can say that genuinely and with complete conviction. Not because it's what I'm supposed to say as a good Christian. Or because I'm in denial. It's because it is what I know and have experienced to be true, particularly over this past year— the most physically, spiritually, and emotionally brutal season that I've ever experienced.

After twenty long years, I can now honestly say my faith is no longer in an outcome. My hope no longer depends upon my healing, but my Healer.

Your wounds may be hidden from the world, but they never escape the notice of a loving God. Through Him, we can find hope—even while we're hurting.

❁

Hope That Heals

*He heals the brokenhearted
and bandages their wounds.*
Psalm 147:3

My Invisible Wound...Bondage
RACHEL'S STORY

Who the world sees...

People probably see me differently now than they would have ten or twenty years ago. Back then people who knew me probably viewed me as a hypocrite. I said I loved God, but often my life and my choices didn't reflect it.

My life is so different now. I'm still flawed. I'm so dependent on God's grace. But He has made a new me. People who meet me now would probably never guess the nature and depth of my past struggle. Today, I hope to be seen as an "air traffic controller," pointing people to a loving God when they veer off course.

What lies beneath the surface...

I accepted Christ as my Savior when I was a young teen. That's when my invisible battle began. My decision to follow Jesus was genuine. However, I had a monster inside of me that was very real, too. And it wanted to destroy me. I come from a long line of generational alcoholism. It permeated my childhood. As a teen, the beast of alcoholism quickly and totally consumed me. It led to a chaotic life of partying and promiscuity.

I never felt good about the life I was leading. I wanted to change. I remember one night in college crying out to God as I laid on my dorm room bed, "This is not who I am, God!" I tried to change, but I slipped back into the same destructive habits. Two months later, I found out I was pregnant. I was an unwed, nineteen-year-old college sophomore. Looking back, I see how God takes the messy pieces of life and makes something beautiful. I loved being a mom.

A few years after my daughter was born, I met my husband. We got married and started a family together. Early in my marriage, I tried to get serious about spending time with God. I stopped partying and getting drunk all the time. But then I started drinking in social situations. I thought I could handle drinking casually. With each drink, the monster inside of me kept demanding, "More! More!" I felt I was in a brutal tug-of-war and the monster was steadily winning.

God began to speak to my heart. I heard Him say, "Lay it down. You are my ambassador." I knew He was telling me to give up my drinking. At the time, I didn't understand what He meant by me being His ambassador. I wanted to lay it down, but the pull of the monster was so strong. The pendulum would swing from one extreme to the other. I would feel God breathing life and strength into me and I wouldn't drink for a while. Then, the pendulum would swing the other way and I would give into my intense craving for alcohol.

When the healing began...

One night, everything came crashing down. It was an extreme evening of drinking and debauchery. I call it the "night of disaster." I can tell you that I nearly brought my entire life to ruin. My choices that night marred all the relationships in my life that I treasured.

I woke up the next morning and clearly remember envisioning myself sitting with my legs dangling over my own grave. My bondage to alcohol and my self-destructive ways had to be broken. I had hit bottom. Satan attacked me relentlessly and made me feel completely worthless. But I wasn't going to give up this time. I wanted sobriety. I had tried so many times before and failed. I couldn't do it on my own. It had taken something incredibly extreme for me to realize how desperately I needed God. I cried out to Him in my despair. This time, I made the choice to fully depend on His power and strength. I had spent my last night indulging the monster.

God showed me that if I would obey and depend on Him, day-by-day, choice-by-choice, He would give me the strength I needed to take the next step of sobriety. He would help me stay sober for good. I also believe He revealed to me that this process of healing was going to take time. He was going to make a whole new me. I had been in bondage for so long.

A few months after the night of disaster, the people I had hurt and damaged so deeply offered me their forgiveness. It was another huge leap in my healing. I felt like a dead branch that was coming to life and about to bud. I remember thinking: *I can breathe. I think I will live. I might even grow.* It accelerated the new life that God had begun in me.

About the same time I was granted forgiveness, I had a powerful dream. In this dream, a man came to my front door. I knew immediately he was a strong and mighty angel. He led me out to my car in the driveway. When he opened the door, two men were inside. They were also angels. A grotesque gremlin was tied up in the back seat. Then I heard a shot. One of the men had killed the gremlin. The angel then led me to the front step of my grandmother's house, where the chain of alcoholism had begun. It was as if God was saying to me, "I'm taking you back where it all began, but we're starting over. The monster is dead."

It has been a long journey. I've had a lot of damage to repair in my relationships. But today, I am free. We all have different "monsters" that we may have been feeding for a long time—pride, selfishness, greed, to name a few. If we will depend fully on God step by step, He will kill that monster and do amazing things in our lives.

How God is using my pain...

It's only in the last year or so that I've been ready to share my story. I understand now what God meant when He assured me that I was His ambassador. So many people struggle with addiction, many times in isolation. As I'm open with my struggle, it really resonates with people. I can connect with and encourage them because I truly understand the pain and desperation of not being able to break free from the habits that are destroying you.

I encourage others to cry out to God in their pain and ask Him for His power. As they do, I know they will experience God moving in their lives. He will enable them to do what they have not been able to do on their own. It's not an easy journey. But as we fully rely on His strength and not our own, He will lead each step of our path to freedom. "It is for freedom that Christ has set us free. Stand firm, then, and do not let yourselves be burdened again by a yoke of slavery." Galatians 5:1 (NIV)

~ As told by Rachel Britz

See the photo at melindameans.com/adorable-photo

CHAPTER 2

Is God Really Good?

'm not sure exactly when the lie took root in my heart. I believe it was early in my chronic pain journey, after several long stretches of agony when I cried out to God and begged for relief. Not even for healing necessarily. But simply a break from my suffering.

And I heard...silence. No response. No immediate rescue from my emotional and physical pain. A divine shrug of the shoulders, if you will, from a God who was supposed to love me.

This thought crept into my mind: If my earthly father had the ability to heal my pain, he would do it in a second. And yet my heavenly Father, who has all the power in the universe, allows me to suffer.

Over the years, that reality messed with my head. It challenged my belief in a God who is truly good. If He could turn a deaf ear to my suffering—and the pain of so many others—time and time again, was He truly compassionate and merciful?

I've heard people say, "You just need to have faith that He's going to heal you." *So, if I'm suffering it's my fault because I don't have enough faith?* That's a heavy load to bear. And I *did* have faith. I *believed* with all my heart that God could heal me. I couldn't accept that *I* was the barrier to my own healing. But that left me back where I started: Wondering why a good God refused to heal my pain.

Sometimes I *am* the cause of my own pain. I've chosen at times to do things my way instead of God's way and I've reaped the consequences. In some cases, suffering can be the result of a spiritual attack. That was certainly true of Job. But sometimes our pain is simply the result of living in a broken, fallen world. This isn't how He intended life to be. Yet God allows tragedy or suffering in our lives for reasons that we just can't always grasp.

From the very beginning of time, Satan has been trying to get us to doubt God's goodness. The fall of man began when he convinced Eve that God was withholding His best from her. Look at what Genesis 3 says:

> The serpent was the shrewdest of all the wild animals the LORD God had made. One day he asked the woman, "Did God really say you must not eat the fruit from any of the trees in the garden?"

Of course we may eat fruit from the trees in the garden," the woman replied. "It's only the fruit from the tree in the middle of the garden that we are not allowed to eat. God said, 'You must not eat it or even touch it; if you do, you will die.'"

"You won't die!" the serpent replied to the woman. "God knows that your eyes will be opened as soon as you eat it, and you will be like God, knowing both good and evil." (v.1-5)

In essence, he asked her, "Is God *really* good? Is He *really* telling you the truth? Is He *really* acting in your best interest?" That's the question we're still wrestling with today: Is God truly good—even when we suffer inexplicable physical, emotional, or spiritual pain? It's an issue we need to settle, friends. Until we do, it will create barriers in our hearts. If we can't fully trust God's love for us, then we can't trust Him period. And no relationship can survive and thrive without trust.

Not How It Was Supposed to Be

When God created the world, it was a thing of beauty. He made a perfect, pain-free, stunningly beautiful place for us to enjoy and care for His creation. He desired for us to have unbroken relationship with Him and to bring Him glory.

God made this world to work in a certain way for our good. He wanted us to love Him as He loved us. He wanted us to *choose* relationship with Him. However, love can't be forced. We can't *make* someone love us. I'm sure we've all tried at some point and found it to be heartbreakingly futile. Real, pure love is a choice. In order to give us that choice, He gave us free will.

Invisible Wounds

Free will opened up the potential for evil. If God allowed us to only make good choices, He would not have given us free will at all. Adam and Eve chose to use that freedom to rebel against God's authority. They thought they knew more about how the world should be than the One who created it.

That sin and rebellion shattered the perfect world God had made. The earth became cursed. We inherited Adam's corrupted nature and now struggle daily with sin. We experience heartache and pain. Disease, sickness, and natural disasters are also consequences of Adam and Eve's fateful choice to do things their way:

> To Adam he said, "Because you listened to your wife and ate fruit from the tree about which I commanded you, 'You must not eat from it,' Cursed is the ground because of you; through painful toil you will eat food from it all the days of your life. It will produce thorns and thistles for you, and you will eat the plants of the field. By the sweat of your brow you will eat your food until you return to the ground, since from it you were taken; for dust you are and to dust you will return." (Genesis 3:17-19 NIV)

Free will inevitably affects other people—either positively or negatively. As a result of other people's selfishness, arrogance, and rebellious choices, we often feel pain and suffering. When we exercise our free will to violate God's laws and original design, natural consequences result.

Why did He create us then? If He knew that we would mess it all up and bring all the problems, chaos, and suffering into the world that we are experiencing today? Author and pastor Lee Strobel explains it this way:

> …many of you are parents. Even before you had children, couldn't you foresee that there was the very real possibility they may suffer disappointment or pain or heartache in life, or that they might even hurt you and walk away from you? Of course—but you still had kids. Why? Because you knew there was also the potential for tremendous joy and deep love and great meaning.[1]

Still, you may be asking, "But God has the power to wipe out all the suffering and evil in this world. Why doesn't He?" He will. He promised us:

"…Look, God's home is now among his people! He will live with them, and they will be his people. God himself will be with them. He will wipe every tear from their eyes, and there will be no more death or sorrow or crying or pain. All these things are gone forever…Look, I am making everything new!" (Revelation 21:3-5)

Strobel goes on to say that God is delaying His return—when all things will be made right—in the hope that more people will put their trust in Him and spend eternity in heaven. In other words, His delay is because He *is* merciful, not because He is uncaring or indifferent. Consider 2 Peter 3:9: "The Lord isn't really being slow about His promise, as some people think. No, he is being patient for your sake. He does not want anyone to be destroyed, but wants everyone to repent."

More Than We Deserve

I'm a good person. I try to do the right things. Good grief, God, I'm serving You! I don't deserve to be in pain like this! This shouldn't be happening to me! I've had those thoughts. Maybe you have, too.

Right now, there is a young family in my church that is going through an incredibly overwhelming and difficult season. They love God passionately. They are always serving others. Several years ago, they added two boys to their family of four through foreign adoption.

After two heart wrenching years—filled with family counseling sessions, individual therapy and much prayer— one of the boys was unable to bond with their family. The reasons were complicated and not the fault of the parents or their new young son. Though it ripped their hearts out, they felt God's unmistakable leading in placing him with another family where he is now doing well. Shortly after this season, their biological son had a retinal detachment and lost most of his sight in one eye. A few months ago, their oldest daughter was diagnosed with a very rare form of pediatric thyroid cancer—prognosis unknown at this time. And as I write, the mother is awaiting surgery to remove her own thyroid, as the doctors suspect she may have cancer as well.

No relationship can survive and thrive without trust.

Humanly, our first thought is to ask, "What? Why?" From our perspective, this family does not deserve this. Shouldn't their good deeds and faith in God inoculate them from this kind of relentless, overwhelming pain and suffering?

Now here is a hard truth, friends. One of those that we'd rather conveniently forget: Living a good life, believing in God is not a "get-out-of-suffering" free card. We don't deserve anything. We aren't entitled to any certain outcome. We aren't entitled to a life without pain and suffering. We deserve death. We deserve nothing.

While we can cling to the belief that our suffering and pain is unfair, let's consider what *true* fairness would be. *True* fairness would be eternal separation from God. After all, from the beginning of time, that is what we've chosen: "For everyone has sinned; we all fall short of God's glorious standard" (Romans 3:23).

But a loving God gave us another choice through the brutal death of His Son Jesus Christ. It is only by the mercy of a loving, compassionate God that we have the hope of redemption:

> Yet God, in his grace, freely makes us right in his sight. He did this through Christ Jesus when he freed us from the penalty for our sins. For God presented Jesus as the sacrifice for sin. People are made right with God when they believe that Jesus sacrificed his life, shedding his blood. This sacrifice shows that God was being fair when he held back and did not punish those who sinned in times past, for he was looking ahead and including them in what he would do in this present time. God did this to demonstrate his righteousness, for he himself is fair and just, and he makes sinners right in his sight when they believe in Jesus. (Romans 3:24-26)

Invisible Wounds

This quote from Tim Keller expresses this beautifully:

> [We ask,] "Why does God allow evil and suffering to continue?" and we look at the cross of Jesus, we still do not know what the answer is. However, we now know what the answer isn't. It can't be that he doesn't love us. It can't be that he is indifferent or detached from our condition. God takes our misery and suffering so seriously that he was willing to take it on himself.[2]

It's a Matter of Trust

God loved us enough to send His Son to die for us. He is worthy of our trust. As we choose to believe God's Word and trust His character, even when we don't feel like it and our circumstances tell a different story, we open the door for the Holy Spirit to do a transforming work in our hearts and lives. Psalm 13 gives us a beautiful picture of what this looks like:

> O Lord, how long will you forget me? Forever?
> How long will you look the other way?
> How long must I struggle
> with anguish in my soul,
> with sorrow in my heart every day?
> How long will my enemy
> have the upper hand?
> Turn and answer me, O Lord my God!
> Restore the sparkle to my eyes,
> or I will die.
> Don't let my enemies gloat, saying,

"We have defeated him!"
Don't let them rejoice at my downfall.
But I trust in your unfailing love.
I will rejoice because
you have rescued me.
I will sing to the Lord
because he is good to me.

The questions, "Does God really love me?" and "Is God really good?" demand satisfactory answers. I've wrestled with them in this chapter, but I'll never be able to explain them in a way that completely addresses all situations and removes all doubt. We can learn about the goodness of God intellectually. It's important for us to continually seek Him and build a solid foundation of truth that we find in His Word. However, these questions can't be fully settled in the mind. A rock-solid trust and assurance of God's goodness is found most powerfully when our growing knowledge of God is confirmed in our experience—when He meets us powerfully and sweetly in the midst of our suffering.

As strange as it sounds to us, the darkness of our circumstances reveals the light of God's hope, love, and goodness. We'll be exploring that in the next chapter.

Hope That Heals

But God is so rich in mercy, and he loved us so much, that even though we were dead because of our sins, he gave us life when he raised Christ from the dead. (It is only by God's grace that you have been saved!)
Ephesians 2:4-5

My Invisible Wound...Loss
LINDSEY'S STORY

Who the world sees...

People think I'm super happy. I'm in ministry and seem outgoing, so they don't readily assume that I have a lot of brokenness.

What lies beneath the surface...

My husband and I have always wanted a big family. So when my son was two years old, my husband and I were thrilled when I became pregnant with our second child. Near the end of the first trimester, we went for an ultrasound and heard the tiny heartbeat and saw it blip across the screen for the first time. That's always such an amazing and reassuring moment. However, a few weeks later, at my next doctor's appointment, the heartbeat was gone. We were devastated.

At the time, I processed it by trying to put a brave face on it. I stuffed my pain. I wanted to be a good witness for God. I wanted to be a good Christian whose faith didn't appear shaken by pain and loss. So I didn't acknowledge or express my anger and disappointment with God.

It seemed like everything was turning around the next year when I had a positive pregnancy test on New Year's Day. We were ecstatic! I immediately thought, "God is going to redeem our pain with a new baby to start out the new year." Then, about *three hours* after that positive test, I began bleeding. I miscarried again.

This is when all the anger and disappointment toward

God that I had stuffed came bubbling to the surface. I couldn't believe that He would allow me to have this positive test, only to miscarry hours later. Why couldn't the bleeding have started the day before? I would never have known I was pregnant. It seemed so cruel. How could He allow that?

I was disillusioned with God, but I didn't know what to do with that. I concentrated on moving forward. In July, I found out I was pregnant again. Everything looked great, but before the first trimester was over, another miscarriage. We quickly decided that we couldn't handle risking the pain and disappointment for a while. We chose to take some time to grieve and process before we decided if we wanted to try again.

A month later, my mom, who lives out of state, called me and asked to Skype with us. This was unusual so I wondered what could be wrong. She explained that there was a young woman from my home church who was seven months pregnant and wanted to choose adoption. My mom wondered if we would be interested in adopting the baby. This was completely out of the blue. At this point we hadn't yet considered adoption. Yet we immediately felt we should do this.

God's activity was evident throughout the entire process. We felt an instant connection the moment we met the birth mother. She asked us what we would name the child. I said, "We're thinking about Caden." She began to cry. She revealed that Caden was the name she had chosen for her son when she was going to parent him.

The adoption process was inexplicably smooth. This was a tribal adoption (Native American) across state lines. It's usually very complicated, but everything fell into place quickly, allowing me to be present at the birth, and for us to take the baby home from the hospital. Incredibly, there are nine different tribes in and around my hometown, and my husband and I both have the same Native American heritage as our baby. What are the chances that everything would fit together so perfectly? Clearly God was in this.

We still wanted to expand our family and decided to try to get pregnant again. About a year after the adoption, we underwent extensive fertility testing. The doctors couldn't find any cause for why I miscarry. They put us on some preventive medications just in case they missed something and encouraged us to try again.

A short time later, we suffered our fourth miscarriage. This one was harder than the other three. I honestly believed that we had gotten our "Why?" when we adopted Caden. Why did God allow our miscarriages? So we could adopt Caden. He was ours. Now, I believed that we wouldn't miscarry anymore. When we did, I became depressed. Focusing on my past miscarriages and the stress of trying to get pregnant stole my joy. I was not able to see or fully appreciate the blessings right in front of me.

The passionate faith that I'd had since I was a preteen fractured. From the beginning, I had a deep love and excitement for God. I ended up going to Bible College and graduated top in my class. I felt like I knew God pretty well. I thought if God loved me He wouldn't let certain things happen to me. Yes, I thought there would be struggles and difficulties, but somehow I thought there was a line He wouldn't cross. A level of pain that He wouldn't allow. One miscarriage? Maybe. But *four*? He would never allow *that* to happen to me. I felt He had violated my trust. I questioned so much of what I had believed about Him.

When my healing began...

With the encouragement of people who loved me, I finally went for counseling. For me, this was key to my healing. I was done stuffing my pain. I was through putting on a happy face. The counselor walked me through my anger, allowing me to verbalize all my raw doubts and emotions without judgment. Getting honest with God was huge for me. My bitterness began to lift as I confessed and worked through my pain with Him.

Healing has been a journey. God is still revealing parts of my heart and mind that need to be transformed. Recently, we became foster parents. The first baby was one we knew we were only going to have for a short while. The second child, however, didn't have any family that was willing to take him. We visited him in NICU and took him home with us. We thought we would be able to start the adoption process. And then the social worker found a cousin who was willing to adopt the baby.

Through that disappointment, God revealed to me that I was fostering for the wrong reasons. Sure, I wanted to help children, but I was also using it to fill a void in me. I sensed that He wanted me to let it go—adopting, trying for more babies—and to just enjoy the children and the life He has given me. Feelings of pain and loss will always be there. But after years of heartache, struggle and disappointment, I'm finally at the place where I'm content with whatever God's plan holds for me.

This journey has stretched my view of God. I've come to terms with the fact that God didn't promise me an easy life. In fact, He promised me the opposite. He only promised that He would never leave me. In the midst of my grief, God has been so kind to give me glimpses of His activity and reassurance of His love.

The day I lost my first baby was October 15th, which happens to be Infant Loss Remembrance Day. Every year we light four candles to remember the lives of the babies we lost. And we know we're not alone. People all over the world are sharing in this and remembering the babies they lost as well.

How God is using my pain...

Watching God use my pain in a powerful way has helped to mend my fractured faith and heal my hurting heart.

I began to get honest with others about my struggles— both verbally and in my writing. As I've shared more openly, I've seen God redeeming my pain. I talk about how God met me over and over again in the middle of my suffering and it encourages others. It helps them to see God in their own pain stories and starts the healing process for them, as well.

~ As told by Lindsey Bell

CHAPTER 3

The Hard Road That Leads To Hope

The greatest faith is born in the hour of despair.
When we can see no hope and no way out,
then faith rises and brings the victory.
~ Lee Robertson

I knew the truth. God promised never to leave me or forsake me, but then why did I feel so abandoned and alone? I was in a terrible state of pain and weariness—the most difficult and exhausting stretch in my nineteen-year-long battle with chronic illness.

I had developed a critical case of anemia that left me so depleted I couldn't walk across my house without becoming out of breath. At the same time, I injured a hip tendon causing a degree and intensity of pain I had never before experienced.

When I was not in the hematologist's office for IV iron infusions, I was receiving multiple painful anti-inflammatory injections into my lower back and hip to relieve my suffering. The injections were not a quick fix.

Invisible Wounds

They left me incredibly sore and nearly unable to walk for several days afterwards. Eventually, they would ease the pain for a little while, but then it would re-intensify and I would go for more excruciating shots.

This double whammy of anemia and hip pain hit me as I was planning a women's conference for my church with the theme "Live Free." I was supposed to give an inspiring message of hope and freedom. The irony was not lost on me. I had never felt so hopeless and in bondage. I couldn't see an end to this nightmare. I didn't know how to live like this. How many times have we heard, "God has a purpose in your pain"? Or "He's got a plan"? Guess what? I didn't care. I didn't care about His purpose. I wasn't keen on His plan. I wasn't interested in learning anything new. I just wanted relief from my suffering.

I cried out to God. Begged Him for mercy. Asked Him why. Wept angry, bitter tears. Demanded answers. But I couldn't seem to feel God's presence. Nothing about my circumstances improved. In fact, it seemed to get worse at every turn. I doubted He even *saw* me in my pain. Over and over again, I questioned His love for me. During that time, I wrote this prayer in my journal:

> Lord, I want to be close to You. I'm just angry at You. Angry that You seem deaf to my cries... I am so weary. So weary. Where are You? You seem to be so removed from my pain—a Cosmic Observer who simply believes pain is part of the human journey, so I should suck it up and be joyful. I'm mad at You... THIS is

not living. THIS robs me of my ability to live my life. How can this be Your will for my life? I want to feel You are tender and care about my pain. But right now... I feel nothing. I don't know that You are listening. I just want to feel like Your precious daughter who You lovingly relieve of pain because You can and because Your love for me overwhelms You. No lessons to teach me. Just love.

Then I went silent. For the first time I can remember, I couldn't pray. I don't mean that I *refused* to pray. I mean that I *could not*. No matter how discouraged or even angry I've been with God, I've always been able to pour out my heart to Him. I have a bookshelf full of prayer journals—the good, the bad and the ugly spilled out on page after page. As my husband has always told me, I'm a good pray-er.

But suddenly I couldn't. My anger and frustration at God had turned to *numbness*. I was worn down by physical and emotional exhaustion. Worn out by all my countless efforts to get well. Disillusioned by years of seeming disregard for my desperate prayers for healing. I was spent. I had nothing left.

Upon the death of his beloved wife, the great Christian author C. S. Lewis struggled in this way, too: "Meanwhile, where is God? This is one of the most disquieting symptoms... But go to Him when your need is desperate, when all other help is in vain, and what do you find? A door slammed in your face, and a sound of bolting and double bolting on the inside."[1]

It is at that point of desperation, when our wounds won't

heal—despite our best human efforts and years of desperate prayers—that we question the truth of God's goodness and mercy because we can't see or feel it. Emotions can easily become our truth. Darkness envelops us. Hope seems lost.

A Crisis of Faith

In essence, we encounter a crisis of faith—one so deep and difficult that it makes us question everything we've believed about the nature of God. St. John of the Cross, in his writing, termed this crisis "the dark night of the soul."

In his book *Emotionally Health Spirituality*, Peter Scazzero describes it as confronting a spiritual Wall in our journey:

> We discover for the first time that our faith does not appear to "work." We have more questions than answers as the very foundation of our faith feels like it is on the line. We don't know where God is, what he is doing, where he is going, how he is getting us there, or when this will be over...It (the Wall) is not simply a one-time event...It appears to be something we return to as part of our ongoing relationship with God.[2]

Scazzero is right. I *had* encountered other dark nights in my journey. However, this past fall, I entered the deepest, darkest night of the soul that I had ever experienced. I was completely consumed with fear, discouragement, and despair.

In the Bible, Jacob had a dark night of the soul much like mine. Jacob had spent twenty years in his father-in-law Laban's home. Laban was a deceitful, difficult man. Those years were contentious and miserable. Finally, God commanded Jacob to return to his homeland—the promised land of Canaan. However, to do so, Jacob had to pass through Edom, the territory of his brother, Esau. Jacob was a deceitful man himself—tricking Esau out of his birthright as the firstborn son and then out of his father's blessing. When Esau realized what Jacob had done, he planned to kill him. Jacob fled and had not seen his brother since. As he neared Edom, Jacob was consumed with fear.

In fact, Jacob sent his family, servants, and possessions across the Jabbok River *first* to meet Esau. Jacob was alone in the camp. Before he could cross over to meet his brother, he encountered another adversary: "…a man came and wrestled with him until the dawn began to break" (Genesis 32:24).

Most scholars agree the "man" who Jacob wrestled was actually the pre-incarnate Christ in human form. This epic battle would exhaust all his human strength and leave him forever changed.

Exposing Our Point of Deepest Need

Jacob had been running from Esau and plagued by fear for years. He had spent nearly his entire life trying to manufacture his own blessings and survival—scheming and plotting to steal his brother's birthright, running and hiding from his wrath, making deals with Laban to get what he wanted. His whole life had been a constant struggle with adversaries. He had somehow been able to survive—and sometimes even thrive—in the midst of it.

Now, confronting his greatest fear, his brother Esau, Jacob

again tried to secure his own deliverance: "... I will try to appease him by sending gifts ahead of me. When I see him in person, perhaps he will be friendly to me. So the gifts were sent on ahead, while Jacob himself spent that night in the camp" (Genesis 32:20-21).

While Jacob's character and reliance on God had grown over the years, he still had a very firm reliance and dependence on his own efforts to save the day. Also, perhaps because of his own past deceptions and depravity, he didn't believe he was worthy of God's blessing. Ultimately, he doubted God would deliver him.

When this "Man" confronted him and wrestled with him, Jacob once again relied on his own strength for survival. He put up an enormous, prolonged, and admirable fight. Finally, the man "touched Jacob's hip and wrenched it out of its socket" (Genesis 32:25). According to Barnes' Notes on the Bible, "The thigh is the pillar of a man's strength...Let the thigh bone be thrown out of joint, and the man is utterly disabled."[3]

> God is sweetly tender in our brokenness.

This is the turning point in the story. "Then the man said, 'Let me go, for the dawn is breaking!' But Jacob said, 'I will not let you go unless you bless me'" (Gen. 32:36). Self-sufficient Jacob was suddenly completely disabled. He could no longer fight on his own strength. He finally, *finally* recognized his own complete helplessness and need. He acknowledged his only hope and strength was in God.

His carnal weapons were lame and useless; they failed him in his contest with God. What he had surmised for the past 20 years now dawned on him: he was in the hands of the One against whom it was useless to struggle. After this crippling touch, Jacob's struggle took new direction. Now crippled in his natural strength, he became bold in faith.[4]

I can so relate to Jacob. For years, I tried very hard to control my disease. I tried to overcome it, time and time again on my own efforts. I believed that if only I took the right medicine, found the right doctor, or ate the right foods, I could regain my health. I prayed, of course, but I acted as if my healing were primarily based on my efforts and my performance. I tried to manufacture my own healing and blessings. I placed my hope in an outcome.

Suddenly, this excruciating hip injury (combined with anemia) had left me completely disabled. I found myself in a place where I could do virtually nothing on my own strength. I could do nothing but be still. I was defeated, helpless, and broken.

I gradually realized with an inexplicable depth of clarity I had never before experienced that my only hope is in God. Doctors had failed me. My own efforts had fallen short, time and time again. All these years, I thought my greatest need was healing. But in reality my greatest need was to confront my own self-sufficiency and allow God to purge the doubt that had for so long permeated my heart: If God truly loved me, He would heal me. He would relieve my pain.

Invisible Wounds

As I lay in bed, God gave me a message called "Invisible Wounds" for the ladies at the Live Free conference. I wrote it partly as therapy—as I wallowed in the depths of desperate pain and complete despair. As I slowly gained this new view of God and He began the process of healing my heart, my talk conveyed the hope and love of a God that is present and fighting for us in the midst of our pain.

On the day of the conference, I was stronger, but still recovering. I could see daybreak, but was still nursing the physical and spiritual wounds of my dark night. I knew God wanted me to deliver this message, but I had no strength. I had barely practiced my talk. When I did, I couldn't get through it without breaking down. My mind and body were deeply weary.

As I waited to go on stage, I breathed a prayer: *God, I can't do this on my own. I have nothing. Whatever happens here today is all You.*

I walked up on stage and experienced the presence and power of the Holy Spirit like never before. I didn't feel the slightest nervousness (not me at all). I barely looked at my notes. Finally, *finally*, I had quit fighting. My confidence was no longer in myself. My hope was no longer in a result. My hope was *Him*.

The God who had seemed so distant and removed from my pain finally felt tangibly present. And He wasn't done yet. After I finished speaking and sat down, women (many audibly weeping) streamed to the altar to pray. I noticed a young woman who I had never met sitting nearby, staring at me. I thought, "She probably wants me to pray with her. I know I should, but I don't know if I can, God."

Before I had a chance to do anything, she touched me on the shoulder, with tears in her eyes and said, "God told me to pray for you and He wants you to know He loves you."

Sweet friends, God will sometimes seem silent as He breaks our pride and shatters our doubts, but He will be sweetly tender in our brokenness. Although the road we're walking sometimes feels like more than we can bear, hold on for the blessing. God is near. Hope is coming.

❋

Hope That Heals

But those who trust in the Lord will find new strength. They will soar high on wings like eagles. They will run and not grow weary. They will walk and not faint.
Isaiah 40:31

My Invisible Wound...Betrayal
BARB'S STORY

Who the world sees...

At one time, I was viewed as someone who pretty much had it all together, in spite of past loss, abuse and pain. I have always been an outgoing introvert. I was often called on to be the "entertainment" for parties and gatherings. Somehow I was always able to put on the silly, comedic, outgoing "hat." I was perceived as the happy, crazy one, but it took every bit of energy and courage I could muster to do it. No one knew that but me. And God.

After my more recent painful experience, I changed. I was no longer the person everyone had known. I was so wounded that for my own sanity, I had to pull back. I became withdrawn and very quiet. The perception of my church and even my friends was that I was far away from God. Little did they know that through that painful time the Lord was my closest friend and I was experiencing a deeper relationship with Him than I had ever had before.

What lies beneath the surface...

Pain and betrayal shattered my world early. When I was just five years old, my mom was in a terrible accident that left her permanently disabled, chronically ill and physically unable to work. My dad was a broken man, unable to function. For the next year my family lived in complete poverty. My siblings and I basically became our own caretakers.

Then my mom died suddenly. The ambulance came to take

her away and I remember chasing after it screaming for them to bring my mom back. On the day of the funeral, my father kissed my brother and me on the cheek and then vanished. We never saw him again. My older siblings were sent to foster care. I never saw them again either. For a few months, family members took care of my brother and me. It did not feel like much of a refuge. We were treated harshly and disciplined if we expressed any pain or grief over losing our mother.

Eventually another family adopted us. We thought we had hit the lottery! It was a nice, stable home. But after a few months, things deteriorated badly. I felt scared and unwanted. My adoptive parents eventually divorced. The instability returned. By this time, I had learned to became a professional 'coper.' I didn't even react anymore. I just learned to deal with it.

After the divorce, my adoptive father was awarded custody of us. I was a deeply wounded, angry teenager. He decided it would be best to send us to a private school. He checked out a few and settled on a Christian school. That was a turning point in my life. Teachers and people at the school made me feel loved. I was very broken and I finally felt like I had some spiritual parents. However, they told me to remember the verse, "Forgetting what is behind and straining toward what is ahead" (Phil. 3:13 NIV). They suggested that I just quit focusing on my past.

So I did. I just pushed it all down.

Years later, I fell madly in love, got married and started a beautiful family. We had the normal challenges and ups and downs, but we had a good marriage. I was happy. For years, I kept my pain stuffed. No one would ever guess the depth of suffering in my past. Then one day, my life began to crumble. I was "set up" and badly betrayed by someone in leadership at the church were I worked. It resulted in the loss of my job. I ended up staying at the church, because I didn't want to leave angry and unresolved. It was not the model that I wanted to set for my kids. I had no one safe to talk with about my feelings of betrayal. And even though I didn't realize it at the time, my past hurts—the ones I'd never dealt with—were making this latest betrayal all the more painful.

When my healing began...

Finally, I went to two women counselors at another church. I started sharing everything with them. They said, "Tell us about your past." It was the beginning of acknowledging these very deep wounds that I had buried. A tremendous amount of healing from my past happened through this experience with these two loving women. As difficult as the betrayal was, I know that this healing would not have happened if that painful experience had not occurred. It sent me for help to heal in ways that I didn't even know I needed.

Part of my healing from this experience was forgiveness. One day, God clearly told me, "You need to ask this person to forgive you." I knew exactly what and who He meant. It seemed crazy. Why did *I* need to ask for forgiveness? But God was prompting me to go to this leader who had betrayed me and ask forgiveness for the anger and bitterness I had been harboring. I did it. This person granted me forgiveness, but didn't ask for mine. Still, it didn't matter. The weight was gone. It was one of the only times I have experienced instant healing. I felt free to leave the church now because I wasn't leaving angry or wounded.

I had confronted my childhood hurts and this latest wound. I felt healthier. Stronger. Betrayal was behind me. Until the day my husband left me. It rocked my world and brought back all the rejection and betrayal of my past. Early on, I resolved that I was not going to talk badly about my husband to my kids or anyone else. I felt so alone in my pain. Those years after my betrayal at my job were my training ground for this new trial and heartache. Because of the healing God did in my heart back then, I was never really angry with Him. I remember just clinging to His Word. I would pray with my Bible open and pour over the Psalms and Isaiah. Over and over again, I would lament and moan like David in the Psalms and then return to what I knew was true about God.

I have seen God be so faithful and sweet to me. I have developed a relationship with Him that's not head knowledge. I had that kind of faith for years. It was all about duty, guilt and obligation. I hadn't given Him access to my heart. Through all this pain, God has transformed my faulty view of Him. He's assured me of my worth. Now I'm motivated by love and a true desire for God's presence, not by guilt. I now have a redeemed, restored spirit. My relationship is based on truth.

I am still healing. I still have bad days. However, I know that I can have a bad day or a bad week and that doesn't mean I have to have a bad life. I still have to go deep in prayer and remember what is true about me. I am not that rejected little girl anymore. I am fully accepted by God.

We can raise our fists in bitterness or we can lift our hands in praise. It's our choice. But when we search for Him with all our hearts, we will find him.

How God is using my pain...

I have always loved speaking to and encouraging women. I've had lots of opportunities to share my story with groups of women all over the country. However, I haven't been seeking those out lately. I've needed to do more healing. If they come, that's great, but I'm not looking for them.

Instead, I've found that God is bringing me more and more opportunities to encourage women one-on-one. I think just by living through the brokenness and being faithful, it draws women to me. I'm at peace with wherever and however God wants to use me. I just want more of Him.

CHAPTER 4

The God Who Sees Me

God loves each of us as if there were only one of us.
~ Augustine

'll never forget it. Even all these years later, it still gives me a sick feeling in the pit of my stomach. We were on a family vacation in Myrtle Beach, South Carolina. My daughter Molly was four and my son Micah was a toddler. A slew of young families were staying at the hotel and enjoying the beautiful beaches. My very social daughter was thrilled to have a never-ending supply of playmates.

On our last day, the beach was so crowded that we struggled to find a patch of sand to spread out our beach blanket. Still, we decided to squeeze in a few, final precious moments by the water before we headed for the long, looooong (did I mention long?) ride home with small children. Finally, it was time to go. My husband Mike began to pack up our stuff. I told Molly to put her toys in the beach bag, and then turned around for a moment to tend to Micah.

Invisible Wounds

When I turned back around Molly was gone. *Gone.* Nowhere to be found. Where was she? How would we find her? Had someone taken her? My heart started racing. I quickly went into full panic mode. I grabbed Micah and walked around, frantically yelling her name. Mike started searching in the opposite direction. Soon other people began to join us in the search.

Then, suddenly, mercifully, there she was. She had noticed one of her favorite playmates a little further down the beach and dashed off to say goodbye—completely unaware of all the commotion she had caused.

As careful as we are as parents, we can't keep our eyes on our children every moment. It's even far more difficult to see what's happening inside their hearts and minds. The same is true of how others see us. As close as we may be to friends and family, they often don't see the *real* us. Parts of ourselves are sometimes too raw, dark, or embarrassing to reveal.

Our Creator sees it all. Every part of us. Every thought, every hurt, every unspoken desire. His loving eye is always on us. He knows us more intimately than we know ourselves. Those painful places we don't want anyone else to see? Those hopes, fears, and doubts we don't dare utter? He wants to meet us there.

In Genesis 16, God saw a woman named Hagar in the midst of her pain and despair. God had promised Abraham a child who He would make into a great nation. When years passed and his wife, Sarai, was old and still not pregnant, she suggested Abraham have a child with her maidservant, Hagar. When Hagar became pregnant, she suddenly felt superior to Sarai—perhaps more favored by God—and routinely disrespected her. In pain and retaliation, Sarai mistreated Hagar so badly that she finally ran away.

As she wandered in the wilderness, Hagar most likely felt alone, fearful, and hopeless. She finally spotted a place of physical refreshment. That is where God met her: "The angel of the Lord found Hagar beside a spring of water in the wilderness..." (Gen. 16:7).

It's in the "wilderness" of our circumstances, either ones beyond our control or those partly or entirely of our own making, that we most readily believe that God has lost sight of us. He must have turned away for a moment and lost us in the crowd. Maybe we feel we don't deserve for Him to see or help us. In truth, the wilderness is often where God wants to reveal Himself to us most sweetly. I love what Hosea 2:14 says: "Therefore I am now going to allure her; I will lead her into the wilderness and speak tenderly to her." (NIV)

The angel of the Lord heard Hagar's cry of distress. Many scholars believe this angel was God, in the Person of Jesus Christ. He assured her that He would take care of her and her unborn son. It would not be easy, but He would give her and her son what they needed. He would create a great nation from her and her son's descendants.

It is at the end of her encounter—strengthened, comforted, and hopeful—that Hagar gave God the name, El Roi, or "The God Who Sees": "...She said, 'You are the God who sees me.' She also said, 'Have I truly seen the One who sees me?'" (Gen. 16:13)

When God sees us, it's not simply observational. It doesn't

mean He just knows *where* we are. When God "sees" us in our pain and misery, it is a supremely loving act. He desires to extend His overwhelming love, mercy, and compassion to us. He wants to comfort and help us in the midst of our quiet desperation and despair.

He Sees Who We Are

In Judges 6, God calls a man named Gideon to lead the Israelites into battle against the Midianites, a powerful enemy that is prepared to destroy them. Gideon wasn't the most likely choice. Look at his response: "But Lord,… how can I rescue Israel? My clan is the weakest in the whole tribe of Manasseh, and I am the least in my entire family!" (Judges 6:15)

But do you know how the Lord addressed Gideon when He came to him? "The Lord is with you, mighty warrior" (Judges 6:12 NIV). He calls him "mighty warrior"! At this point do you know how many battles Gideon had led? Zero. Zip. None. Nada. But God saw who Gideon truly was. He knew a warrior lurked inside Gideon. He wants us to see ourselves the way He sees us.

Growing up, I saw myself very much like Gideon. I didn't feel like anyone special. I am the youngest in my family. I was shy, fearful, and unsure of myself. I certainly didn't feel equipped to fight lengthy battles of chronic illness and pain. I didn't feel prepared to meet difficult, sometimes overwhelming, challenges in my family life.

Slowly and patiently, He has revealed and built qualities of character, endurance, and perseverance in me. I thought I was weak. But over many years and many battles, He has helped me realized that I truly am a mighty warrior. Not because of my strength, but because of *His*.

People sometimes ask me, "How do you do it? You've had so much to deal with. I could never go through what you have." Guess what? Neither could I. Here's what I've learned: When we are able to endure long, difficult trials and wounds, we see that our faith is real. We realize we couldn't possibly do this on our own strength.

Since I have been more open with my pain, I have received so much support. I have people who now regularly pray for me. I can feel those prayers. I would never go back to those days of lonely isolation. However, while before I felt like no one saw my pain, I sometimes feel like now that's *all* they see. It threatens to become "who I am."

> Our Creator sees it all. Every thought, hurt and unspoken desire.

I have to remind myself regularly that my struggle is not my identity. It's not yours either, friend. "The God Who Sees" does not look at you or me as someone with problems and pain. He simply sees someone He loves deeply. He sees the *real* us—who He made us to be. Who we can be when we draw on His power. He sees us with His gentle eyes of love and redemption.

Not Just a Face in the Crowd

So many times over the years, I have identified with the woman with the issue of blood in Mark 5: "A woman in the crowd had suffered for twelve years with constant bleeding. She had suffered a great deal from many doctors, and over the years she had spent everything she had to pay them, but she had gotten no better. In fact, she had gotten worse. She had heard about Jesus, so she came up behind him through the crowd and touched his robe. For she thought to herself, 'If I can just touch his robe, I will be healed'" (Mark 5:25-28).

Like me, she desperately wanted a result—the relief of her terrible problem of bleeding. Instantly, her body was healed: "Immediately the bleeding stopped, and she could feel in her body that she had been healed of her terrible condition" (Mark 5:29).

Result achieved.

But if the story had ended there, it would have been tragically incomplete. Under Jewish law, a woman with an issue of bleeding was considered unclean. Anything or anyone she touched was also considered unclean. This meant that she couldn't touch her husband or children. She probably didn't live with them. She couldn't worship in the synagogue. She was ostracized from society. She had most likely not felt the warmth of human touch for many years. Physical healing did nothing to touch the deep pain of years of shame, rejection and isolation. It didn't cure her need for a Savior.

Mark tells us that a huge crowd was all around Jesus. The woman came up *behind* Him. But Jesus still "saw" her. She was not just a face in the crowd. Jesus realized at once that healing power had gone out from him, so he turned around in the crowd and asked, 'Who touched my robe?'" (Mark 5:30)… he kept on looking around to see who had done it" (v.32).

Did Jesus know who had touched Him? Of course. He called her out not to shame her, but to relieve her of her shame. He wanted to acknowledge her deep suffering. He wanted her to know she truly was healed. He wanted the crowd to know that she was no longer unclean. Jesus didn't want this woman to believe she stole her healing. He had freely given it. He didn't want her to think that His garment had healed her, but that her Savior had.

"Then the frightened woman...came and fell to her knees in front of him and told him what she had done. And he said to her, 'Daughter, your faith has made you well. Go in peace. Your suffering is over'" (Mark 5:33-34).

In Sheila Walsh's book, *The Storm Inside Study Guide*, she writes:

> If the woman had just touched Jesus' clothes, been healed, and slipped away unnoticed, she might have thought she was accessing impersonal magical power...She might also have carried her shame home with her, even though the bleeding has stopped. Jesus offered her the opportunity to come to Him face to face, person to person.[1]

It is not through the *result* that the most important transformation comes. It is through the *relationship* with Jesus. He changed her external circumstances. But it's when He draws her near, assures her that He sees her, acknowledges her faith, and relieves her shame that true healing occurs. She leaves a different woman because He calls her "daughter."

Invisible Wounds

Our encounters with Jesus always leave us changed. As we seek Him, we find the healing that we long for. It just may not look like what we envisioned. In chapter two, I wrote about my recent "dark night of the soul." During that time, I shared my desperate struggle and despair with my sweet friend, Mary.

I told her about my most recent doctor appointment. I had just had an extensive panel of testing done. When I sat down for him to go over my results, he said this: "I have no idea how you are functioning as well as you are and looking as good as you do. If I didn't know you and only went by your test results, I would expect you would come into my office in a wheelchair."

In my mind, it was further evidence that God was not present in my struggle. He didn't see me. As I poured out my pain, Mary wasn't judgmental or condemning. She shared in my tears and frustration. Then she said something that became one of the breakthroughs in my battle: "Melinda, don't you see? God *has* been present. You should be in a wheelchair! But despite your ongoing health issues, He has given you the power to be a wife and a mother, to care for a special-needs child, to write a book, and be in full-time ministry. Consider all you have been able to do—that is the power of God working through you."

She continued, "I don't know why He is allowing you to go through this terrible stretch right now, but I do know this: This period of your life is *anointed*. God will bring victory out of this pain."

All these years, as I have been desperately clinging to the hem of His robe, He *had* been giving me His power. He did see me. I was not forsaken. He hadn't left me. Although I haven't always recognized it, day by day, moment by moment, He has given me what I've needed to overcome my pain, my emotions, my doubts. Time after time, He has sweetly given me reminders of His love and assurance of His provision.

The God Who Sees Me sees you, too. He loves each of us as if there were only one of us.

✻

Hope That Heals

You keep track of all my sorrows. You have collected all my tears in your bottle.
You have recorded each one in your book.
Psalm 56:8

My Invisible Wound...Feeling Unloved
GRACE'S STORY

Who the world sees...

The world sees a wife, a mom. I always appear happy, upbeat and positive—a passionate prayer warrior who is heavily involved in helping people at work and church. Some of my co-workers would probably say that I'm "that annoying Jesus lady at work."

What lies beneath the surface...

For most of my life, I felt like I was crazy and disconnected. I was afraid to get close. I had a sense of confusion. I didn't understand why I had so much hate. I was always trying to connect to people, but had no idea how to connect to myself. I understand now that this stemmed from being sexually abused at a very young age. Other circumstances in my childhood only compounded my pain and the lies I believed about myself. Poor choices and dysfunctional relationships became the pattern of my life.

Growing up, I was one of eight children. One of my siblings was born with special needs. I remember trying so hard to get any attention at all from my mother. Poor thing had her hands so full with life. Teenagers, a preteen and a child with a disability...I look back now and think she deserves a medal! Providing for a huge family and running a business became very stressful for my father also. He is such a different man today, but back then the strain and pressure often made him angry and difficult to be around.

As a child, I was made fun of because my house was old and dirty and I was poor. I remember wanting to fit in so badly, but I felt so damaged and different from my peers. As a young child, I had repeated nightmares of being violated. I even had nightmares of Jesus hurting me. How could I love this Jesus that hurts me in my nightmares? I would scream in my pillow for them to go away and pull out my hair just to make my mind stop thinking.

Then, as a preteen, a fire destroyed our home. Overnight, we lost almost everything. My sisters went to live with relatives. My parents lived in a tent on our property to protect what was left of our belongings. I had to go with my brother to live with family friends and help out with my baby nephew. As I look back, it was way too much responsibility for a young girl. Homeless, living away from my family and taking care of a baby...I was just trying to make everyone happy.

When the dust finally settled, the nightmares were back. I was in middle school. I didn't want to be damaged anymore. I just wanted to belong. Because I was always one of the youngest in my class, I mostly hung around with older kids. When I was thirteen, my best friend suggested I have sex. I figured it might help the nightmares to subside. I became sexually active just after my fourteenth birthday. I began to fill with hate. I hated myself, hated my parents and tied all my worth to a guy who left me for my best friend. So now I hated him.

This unfortunately was the beginning of me giving my heart to everyone except our loving Father. I had more empty relationships. They used me but I always allowed it. I felt I was worth nothing, so I allowed people to treat me like I was worth nothing. At sixteen, I became friends with a girl who took me to a Christian youth conference. I had accepted Jesus as a child. Now I rededicated my life to Him. I was so pumped about missions that I went to Haiti one summer as a teen missionary. I knew I loved Jesus. I was just missing the most important component: that He loved me.

Not long after that summer, I met another boy and became pregnant. I was scared, but...a baby! I thought someone was finally going to love me unconditionally! I married the father a few months later. We had an incredible first year of marriage. Then, because of deep dysfunction—his and mine—our marriage began to fall apart. By this time in my life, I was struggling with raging bulimia. I miscarried our second child. I became very depressed. A few months later I found out I was pregnant again. When my daughter was born, the nightmares came back, except now with a terrible daytime fear. I lived in obsessive fear that someone would hurt my children. I had lost my mind.

Our marriage was characterized by the insanity of doing the same things over and over and expecting different results. My husband confessed he was having an affair, but eventually ended it. I still wanted my marriage to work so badly. I wanted to be loved! I was so co-dependent on this dysfunctional relationship. Then one day I just gave up. Instead of turning to Christ, I turned to another man. I proceeded to have an affair that tore two families apart. I hurt so many people and also became pregnant by this man. I was in such a deep depression.

I believed God's love was performance-based. If I was

doing good things, maybe I was on God's good side and He could love me. If I was doing bad, I believed God was mad at me. I felt He was mad at me a lot. I was too weak to stand up for my unborn child or myself. I had an abortion. The pain of that abortion lingered within my soul. I needed God, but I felt I had crossed the line. I had gone too far for Him to love me. I ended the affair and decided to give it one more shot with my then-husband. It didn't work. I had to make the very difficult decision to end my marriage. Shortly after that, my mom passed away. I lost my home. I didn't know what to do.

When the healing began...

In desperation, I started going to a study group at church. Through this class, God gradually peeled the blinders from my eyes. The pattern of my life sickened me. It had to stop. I had been addicted to chaos my whole life. Whenever things began to calm down, I ran out and found some more chaos. One night, I asked my brother why I always seemed to make bad choices. I really didn't mean to. He told me that it was because I hadn't surrendered every bit of my life to Christ. I was so angry and offended. I believed that God took my marriage, my house, my mother and my mind. I thought there was nothing left to give Him! But my brother wasn't talking about earthly things. He was talking about surrendering my heart. Jesus wanted my whole heart.

I was living with a wonderful man at the time. But I knew in my spirit that Christ was convicting me to have him move out until we were married. He reluctantly agreed. It was hard, but I knew I had to start surrendering my whole life and heart, not just part of it. One day, I was so depressed that I called out sick from work. I was lying in my bed. I had given up on life. I was done with the cycle of my own behaviors. I had no idea how to change. As I lay there damaged and desperate, I heard Jesus whisper in my ear: "Grace, I love YOU, no matter what." For the *first time*, I internalized that truth. In that single moment, I gave him all my baggage I have carried over all the years. I got up, took a shower and I have been on fire since. Since that day, I have had peace.

I've been hurt and I have hurt many people. But I can't drive forward if I keep looking in the rearview mirror. My recovery has consisted of a lot of falling down and getting back up, a lot of pushing away the very people that I needed most. I still live with some of the consequences and pain of my poor choices. Every day, I am learning how to walk forward in this life because I know I am called for a much greater purpose that I could have ever imagined. That wonderful man who moved out is now my husband. I strive to daily live out a godly example for my children. Today, I can look in the mirror and know I'm not damaged. I am loved…no matter what.

How God is using my pain…

I mentor young girls at my church so they know the love of Jesus and can maybe avoid the mistakes that I made. I have led abortion recovery groups. I am absolutely blown away by how God gives me one-on-one opportunities daily to share my story and encourage women who feel alone and damaged, just like I did for so many years.

CHAPTER 5

Embracing The Race We've Been Given

> Occasionally, weep deeply over the life you
> hoped would be, grieve the losses, then wash your
> face, trust God and embrace the life you have.
> ~ John Piper

Our sweet baby boy had been sick for months. Throwing up constantly. Unable to gain weight. Finally we had an answer: Micah had cystic fibrosis, a genetic, progressive disease that impedes digestion and damages the lungs. Within twenty-four hours of his diagnosis, he was admitted to All Children's Hospital in Tampa, Florida. They needed to stabilize his condition and give us a crash course on how to care for him. I'll never forget walking down that darkened hallway toward his room, numb and shell-shocked.

The next morning the doctor took a lot of time explaining Micah's diagnosis and treatment protocols. I was too overwhelmed to process or remember much of it at the time. But I've never forgotten the words he left us with: "I know how devastating and difficult this all seems right now. But later,

Invisible Wounds

I want you to take a walk down these hallways. This might surprise you, but I don't think you'd want to trade Micah's diagnosis for anyone else's here."

I've thought of his words so many times over the years. As I walk out this path with Micah. As I deal with my own disease and chronic pain. When we're hurting, when our circumstances seem overwhelming or never-ending, we want to escape. Our tendency can be to compare someone else's plight to our own and decide their race is a cakewalk compared to ours. That life would be easier or better if only we could trade our current and personal brand of deep pain or difficulty for her "problems" (insert sarcasm).

I know. I've been there. Yesterday, in fact. I'll probably be there again today. It's a thought process that I battle and turn over to God again and again. When God makes ministry assignments and gets to the chronic pain/illness category, no one would shoot up their hand and shout, "Oh, oh…Pick me, pick me!"

I would never have chosen this race for my son or myself. I have often wished that I didn't have the personal, heart-wrenching experience with chronic pain and illness that has made me well suited to minister to others in pain.

I've actually been angry with other people for having the nerve to be happy. I've had thoughts like, *Oh sure, she's happy and carefree. Why not? She has it easy.* (Often not true, by the way).

Complaining is dangerous, friends. It hardens our hearts. It blinds us to God's provision and sweetness in our pain. It robs us of the power and strength He wants to give us.

Bitterness comes from not getting the life we want—the life we often think we deserve—and then blaming God for it.

So am I saying we aren't ever supposed to feel sad or frustrated or overwhelmed? We can't ever complain? In Dr. Benjamin T. Mast's book, *Second Forgetting*, he explains a much more powerful, productive alternative to grumbling and complaining:

> Groaning and grumbling can seem similar, but biblically they are quite different. Both are responses to suffering, but their sources and their direction are different. Groaning is a response to the weight of suffering, and it is directed toward God as an honest expression of pain, grief, and sorrow. Grumbling also reflects the weight of suffering, but it springs from anger and resentment toward God. It lacks a memory of his past faithfulness. Groaning expresses an element of hope in God, despite current sufferings, but grumbling reflects a lack of hope and faith and is accompanied by a sense of doom. In the Bible, we see that God responds to groaning with mercy, but he responds to grumbling with anger and discipline. Still, even when we grumble there is hope. God is slow to anger, he does not forget his promises, and even in his discipline his goal is to draw his people to him in grace and pardon.[1]

Groaning is holy, grumbling is not. We have to know where to take our pain and frustration when the race feels too long and difficult. When we do, He gives us the ability to embrace the race we've been given.

Submitting to His Plan

Let's revisit the story of Hagar in Genesis 16. Hagar was crushed and weary from the weight of her circumstances. She fled from the cruel mistreatment of Sarai. She was pregnant, alone and wandering in the wilderness, trying to get back to her homeland. As we saw in chapter four, God met her there. "The angel said to her, 'Hagar, Sarai's servant, where have you come from, and where are you going?'" (Genesis 16:8).

Notice that God specifically calls Hagar, "Sarai's servant." This was not without purpose. He was reminding her of Sarai's authority over her. When she admits she is running from Sarai, "The angel of the Lord said to her, 'Return to your mistress, and submit to her authority'" (Genesis 16:9). The angel of God was calling Hagar to a place of humility and submission.

I can only imagine how hard these words were for Hagar to hear. But then God gave her this promise and assurance: "I will give you more descendants than you can count" (Genesis 16:10). He would not abandon her. He would bless her. If He called her to go back to Sarai, He would give her what she needed to persevere.

So many times, God has gently, but clearly reminded me of my position. He's reminded me of His authority. He's convicted me of my attitude and challenged me to submit to where He has me right now. Even though I haven't been real wild about where I am or where He seemed to be taking me.

I take comfort in knowing that Jesus—both fully God and

fully human—struggled with God's will, too. In the Garden of Gethsemane, He also wanted simple deliverance: "My Father! If it is possible, let this cup of suffering be taken away from me." But then He followed it with this: "Yet I want your will to be done, not mine" (Matthew 26:39).

It reminds me that it is an act of my will—powered by the Holy Spirit—to submit to God's will, even when it means I won't see an immediate rescue from my pain. Or perhaps not the rescue that I have in mind.

If anyone had a race that was difficult to embrace, I'd guess it was the apostle Paul. God's plan and ministry for him included beatings, ridicule, isolation, and imprisonment. And that doesn't even include the "thorn in the flesh" that Paul talks about in 2 Corinthians 12:7: "…I was given a thorn in my flesh, a messenger of Satan, to torment me." (NIV)

The Bible doesn't tell us the nature of the thorn. It may have been physical, spiritual, or emotional. As we discussed in chapter two, there can be many reasons for our pain: natural consequences of our own actions, the result of living in a broken and fallen world, or spiritual attack. Sometimes God allows pain in our lives for reasons we don't understand.

In Paul's case, God allowed this "thorn" in Paul's life— one that Satan meant to disable Paul—to accomplish His purposes in Paul's life and ministry. God was using him in powerful and amazing ways. It says in 2 Corinthians 12:7 that God was giving Paul "wonderful revelations." We think of Paul as being superhuman, but he was as vulnerable to pride as any of us. If we look at the beginning of verse 7, Paul says the thorn was given "… in order to keep me from becoming conceited" (NIV). Pastor and author Alan Redpath says this:

"…sometimes the most radiant face hides great pressures, and often the man who is being most blessed of God is being most buffeted by the devil."[2]

Paul pleaded with the Lord repeatedly to remove the thorn. How did God answer? It tells us in verse 9: "But he said to me, "My grace is sufficient for you, for my power is made perfect in weakness." (NIV) Notice that God doesn't say my grace "will be" sufficient for you. He said it "is"—present tense. Right now. In this moment. In every moment. And not just for Paul. For all of us.

Paul had a choice to make. Either he could submit to God's answer, or turn to anger and bitterness. Like Jacob and Hagar, his hardships and difficulties had brought him to the end of himself. He knew he didn't have the strength to persevere on his own power. That realization brought him to a place where he could say this: "Therefore I will boast all the more gladly about my weaknesses, so that Christ's power may rest on me. That is why, for Christ's sake, I delight in weaknesses, in insults, in hardships, in persecutions, in difficulties. For when I am weak, then I am strong" (2 Cor. 12:9-10 NIV).

> His grace is sufficient. In this moment. In every moment.

Consider what preacher Donald Grey Barnhouse said: "We must be triumphant exactly where we are. It is not a change of climate we need, but a change of heart. The flesh wants to run away, but God wants to demonstrate His power exactly where we have known our greatest chagrin."[3]

One Step at a Time

It's one of my favorite scenes from Indiana Jones and the Temple of Doom. "Indy," an archeologist who searches for hidden treasures, reaches the edge of a cliff and confronts a huge, deep chasm in his search for the Holy Grail (the cup that Christ drank from during the Last Supper). As terrifying as it seems, He must find a way to cross the chasm in order to reach the grail on the other side. The journey is especially urgent because his father is dying nearby. The Holy Grail's believed healing powers is the only chance to save his life.

But there is no way forward. Only nothingness. No bridge. No secure path forward. Indy looks at the chasm and says, "Impossible. Nobody can jump this."

Just then, his father yells to him, "You must believe, boy. You must believe." Indy takes a deep breath, looks at the frightening expanse of the chasm, and voices his realization: "It's a leap of faith."

Trembling, he lifts one foot up and steps out into the nothingness. His fear hasn't left him. He just realizes that staying where he's at may be more costly than taking a leap of faith. As soon as he does, a bridge miraculously appears beneath his feet.

Our race feels a lot like that at times. As we carry these invisible wounds, the path ahead can seem impossible. We feel paralyzed. At times, we believe we lack the courage to keep moving forward. We look for solid ground, but only see nothingness. We don't see God. We only see the chasm that lies between where we are and our salvation.

Invisible Wounds

God lovingly whispers to us, "You must believe." Not in our sufficiency, but in His.

Do I fully understand why I've been called to this journey? No, not always. But if I trust the One who is leading it, I don't have to. I only have to follow. Obedience is just taking the next step, trusting that one step at a time He will provide solid ground underneath our shaky feet.

Ultimately, we all have the same choice Paul had: We can spend our time fighting our reality and wishing we had someone else's or we can run the race set before us. The first option leaves us exhausted and leads us nowhere. The second is beyond difficult at times, but is full of God's sweetness amidst the sorrow and His provision, power, and purpose along the path.

The One who leads your journey is trustworthy, my friend. Run your race.

❋

Hope That Heals

*The Lord says, "I will guide you along the best pathway for your life.
I will advise you and watch over you."*
Psalm 32:8

My Invisible Wound... Shattered Dreams
HANNAH'S STORY

Who the world sees...

When I was going through my divorce, people would say, "But you were the perfect couple!" or "You had it all!" I didn't want to attract unwelcome drama or gossip into my life, so only those closest to me knew the full story. I was fortunate to have an awesome family and a couple of godly, supportive girlfriends to walk me through it. Recently, I remarked to one of them, "a very wise woman once told me, 'you never know what happens behind closed doors.'" She nodded her head. Then I reminded her that *she* was that wise woman.

What lies beneath the surface...

My whole life I have been a planner. I had dreams and a plan to achieve them. I went to college where I met the love of my life. He was from a strong, intact family, like my own. I had always planned to marry someone with an intact family because I knew it drastically improved my chances of having a successful marriage. We got married and I completed graduate school. My dream life was underway!

Once we felt financially stable, we were anxious to start a family and fill our home with children. Only nothing happened. For five long years, we prayed for a baby, hoped for a baby, longed for a baby, waited and waited and waited for a baby, but no baby. This was not part of the dream. After many fertility treatments, our savings was gone and still no baby. Then one day, my prayers were answered. I was pregnant!

Invisible Wounds

I was so grateful for this child. I carefully decorated a beautiful, perfect nursery and dreamed of the day we would bring her home from the hospital. Shortly before my due date, a tornado hit our neighborhood. We were safe. However, we now suddenly had a view of the sky where our ceiling used to be. We had to find a place to live while our home was being put back together. Then I developed complications and had an unplanned cesarean section. I dreamed of bringing our precious daughter home to a beautiful nursery. Our home in shambles, we brought her "home" to a hotel instead. Nothing was going according to my plan.

During those first months of motherhood, I was alone a lot. My husband was working long hours. Living away from home meant my friends weren't close by. I was depressed and emotional. Thankfully, my doctor prescribed me some antidepressants and connected me with resources for postpartum depression. I read a book that discussed the circumstantial factors that increased the risk for developing postpartum depression. I think I had most of them. I dreamed that everything from childbirth to motherhood was going to be a wonderful, fulfilling experience that completed me. At that point, everything felt more nightmarish than blissful.

Slowly things improved. We moved back into our home. I even began to hope for more children. I began to connect with other moms and make new friends. However, about the time everything had stabilized and motherhood seemed grand, some other changes were taking place. My relationship with my husband felt like it was deteriorating. I prayed and did everything I could think of to save my marriage. I discovered that in addition to having an addiction problem, my husband was having an affair. We started going to counseling. As I obsessed over phone logs and emails, I discovered my husband was having *multiple* affairs. I prayed and prayed for God to save my marriage. Well, that didn't happen. My husband's promises to change were never kept. My dream of a happy marriage and a big family with the man I loved was dying a slow and painful death.

I knew that the longer my daughter observed our dysfunctional relationship, the more likely she was to model it one day in her own life. It terrified me. I wanted to prevent her from having her heart broken like mine. I wanted her to live a life of integrity with a man of integrity. I knew that she was more likely to be a healthy adult if she had a healthy mother. So when my daughter started school, I began working full-time again and we moved out of the house. I don't believe in divorce, yet after a twelve-year marriage, I was divorced. Yet, I'm at peace that the choices I made and continue to make are in my daughter's best interest.

Throughout this painful journey, my view of God mostly remained positive. Being a mother changed my view of God more than my divorce. Having a child made me understand love on a much deeper level. I better understand how much God loves me and will do anything for me. I recognize that sometimes a "no" answer to my vastly disappointed child could be like the "no" or "not right now" answer God gives me. Sometimes His "no" is for my own protection.

Invisible Wounds

It's sad that sometimes Christians don't always reflect the unwavering love and mercy of the God that I know. All these years later, I still feel looked down upon as an outcast by some people from the church. Being a divorced woman who doesn't tell everyone her "justification" for a divorce sometimes makes me feel judged.

When my healing began...

My healing process actually began through worship and therapy while I was still married. I was fortunate that I had time to pray, process, and become one hundred percent confident of where I needed to go before I got a divorce. Moving out made me feel like I could breathe for the first time in years. I'm a horrible singer and can't carry a tune, but singing to worship music at church, while I was out running, or driving in the car was a key element in my healing process. Reading the Psalms was very comforting, too. I always had the perspective that people around me and people in the Bible struggled much more than I did, making my journey bearable even when I thought it was unbearable.

On the other hand, healing is an ongoing process. Even though I was divorced nearly a decade ago, there are times when the wounds are more painful and exposed than I think they are or should be. The pain sometimes reemerges at unexpected times.

My daughter still wants to know why we are divorced and my answers have not appeased her. At what point, if ever, does she need the gory details? When she pushes, sometimes it hurts. Like a burn victim, whose skin grafts heal, but remain tender to the touch years later, I think our deep hurts can heal, but may never completely disappear.

My "planner" nature also helped in my healing. I asked myself questions like, *What stabilizing factors do I have in my life? What do I* need *to have? What do I want my life to look like? What steps do I need to take to get there?* Then I took those steps. I joined a Bible study, prayed more, regularly made plans to get together with friends, exercised and made time for the things that were most important to me.

My heart had been so broken; I doubted if I could ever give it away again. Then I met a sweet man named Mark. Cautiously, I began to date him, but didn't introduce him to my daughter until many months later. Eventually, we both fell in love with Mark as deeply as he fell in love with us. We married seven years after our first date. Yes, seven years—a long time by most people's standards. It took me that long to get past the emotional scar tissue and feel ready to fully commit again. I wanted to wait until the initial "in love" feelings were not as intense. That way, I could see more clearly if Mark had the character I needed in a lifetime relationship. Our relationship is totally different than my first marriage. Sometimes I feel like my first marriage was a show for the world, only I didn't know it. So much of what I did was for the external approval of others. My needs weren't allowed or acknowledged. I didn't even know what I needed. This relationship is more honest, real, and definitely not a show. I know without a doubt that he genuinely and forever loves my daughter and me.

Invisible Wounds

How God is using my pain...

I'm not always exactly sure how, or if, my pain is being used. Maybe I don't recognize it at times. I may not fully know how God is using it until I see Him one day. I do know that it's given me a less judgmental view of other people. I can't judge someone when I haven't walked in his or her shoes. My pain has helped me become a better person, a better parent, and a better worker at my job. Instead of first reacting to people, I'm much better now at listening, really hearing, and empathizing.

CHAPTER 6

Beauty In Our Brokenness

Behind every exquisite thing that existed,
there was something tragic.
~ Oscar Wilde

I was down to the last few weeks of planning a big event as part of my job. At that point, everything gets crazy and frantic, no matter how well you plan. Suddenly, out of nowhere, I was hit with an inexplicable recurrence of my chronic lower back pain. I had thoughts like, *Really, God? Aren't my normal levels of pain enough? What could possibly be the good or the purpose of this pain, right now?*

When it wouldn't respond to self-care measures, my doctor referred me to a physical therapist. I liked him from the very beginning. He was kind of a tough guy, but caring and funny—just the kind of "medicine" you need from a provider when you're in pain. He asked me what I did for a living. I told him I was an author and women's director at my church. He seemed intrigued and began asking me some random questions about my church, my writing, and my faith.

Invisible Wounds

He explained that he was Jewish. He believed in God, but didn't really go to church. He had big problems with believing Jesus was the Messiah. We had some interesting dialogue about Jesus' life, trial, and crucifixion. He seemed interested in it all, but more as an intellectual exercise than anything else.

Then a few sessions went by without much discussion about the spiritual. But at my last therapy session, he was telling me some stories of his wild youth. Then, he said, "I really was a nice Jewish boy."

Without even thinking, I said, "Jesus was a nice Jewish boy, too."

"Yes, He was." He thought for a moment and then said, "Let's talk about that."

Somehow, he seemed interested in this topic in a different way. I sensed that Holy Spirit was up to something.

He began asking deep, thoughtful questions. I was able to answer them in ways that I know that I don't have the ability to do—on my own. Although my sessions were only thirty minutes long, his next patient "happened" to cancel ("rarely happens," he told me). So for forty-five minutes, we had this incredible exchange where I laid out the entire message of salvation through the death and resurrection of Jesus Christ.

Finally, he said, "I have another Christian friend who hits me over the head with this stuff. He gets so angry. But today, hearing it from you, you are so passionate and so sure, but you're not angry. You just really believe."

"I do."

"Do they talk about stuff like this at your church?"

"Yep. They sure do. Do you want to come?"

"You know what? *Yes*. I'm coming to church." He went out to the other room and told all the other therapists, "I'm going back to church!"

As I left, he said, "I just wish I could be as sure as you are."

I reminded him of the verse in Jeremiah that says, "You will seek me and find me when you seek me with all your heart."

This "tough guy" with tears in his eyes gave me hug. A few days later, I stopped by the office and left a few apologetics books for him at the front desk.

Unfortunately, I haven't seen my new friend at church. But not for one moment do I think that our meeting and our conversations were a coincidence. Maybe he went to another church. I don't know what happened in his heart that day. I do know that encounter was real, divinely appointed, and significant. We both knew it. I also know that if he continues to search, he will find Truth. In the meantime, God will pursue him personally and passionately—just as He does each of us.

> God can bring beautiful circumstances from our pain.

I don't believe God caused my back pain, but I know He used it to bring about His purposes. It made my pain a little easier to bear. I was even grateful for it. As we realize that God truly sees us and loves us—sweetly and personally—it changes our perspectives. When we embrace our race and submit to His plan, we can more fully and clearly recognize and appreciate God's activity in our pain and the beauty He wants to bring out of our brokenness.

Invisible Wounds

Beauty can come from an encounter with a gentle tough guy who needs to hear about the love of Jesus. Or a hurting soul who needs our understanding. Maybe our pain and brokenness can be a powerful conduit for God to express His love, comfort, and healing. In truth, examples of God's redemptive power in our pain are weaved throughout the entire Bible. Each chapter in this book has illustrated how He can work through our hurts. Here are a few more beautiful gifts that pain can bring us:

It can lead us to our destiny.

I have been involved in some form of women's ministry for years. The past few years I have mainly written and spoken to mothers. I've loved it. Over and over again, I have been frustrated to the point of tears by the way my physical limitations seemed to handicap my ability to accomplish the dreams and passions that God put in my heart. It seemed cruel. Why give me a ministry and a great desire to do it and then allow a condition that repeatedly hindered my abilities?

I wondered how I could continue with the constant struggles and pain. Then, through a series of events over this last year, I had a moment of amazing clarity. When I was ready to hear it, I believe the Holy Spirit whispered to my heart, "This IS your ministry." I was being led to a broader audience: encouraging, writing, speaking and praying for *all* hurting and broken women. I realized for the very first time that my ministry was actually enhanced—not handicapped— by my physical struggles. My pain gave me compassion and empathy. It thwarted my tendency for self-sufficiency. It perfectly equipped me for encouraging others with invisible wounds. I saw the beauty in my pain. Over and over He reminds me of His promise: "My grace is sufficient for you" (2 Corinthians 12:9 NIV).

Since then, along with two other ladies from my church, I have started a chronic illness and caregiver group at my church called Living Hope. For almost a year now, a group of six to ten of us have met weekly to share our burdens, celebrate our victories, and pray for each other. Like me, some women have never spoken openly about their pain. They've never had the opportunity to be in a group of women who really "get" their struggles. Being understood and supported has often had a ripple effect in their families. It's sparked their emotional and spiritual healing.

It can shape our character.

I think of Joseph in the Old Testament. Joseph wasn't the most humble guy. He was clearly his father's favorite, which already made him disliked by his brothers. Then, Genesis 37:2 tells us he "reported to his father some of the bad things his brothers were doing." He tattled on them. Always appreciated by siblings. As if that weren't enough, he bragged to his brothers about a dream he had—how they would all bow down to him one day. Dislike of Joseph turned into hatred: "His brothers responded, 'So you think you will be our king, do you? Do you actually think you will reign over us?' And they hated him all the more because of his dreams and the way he talked about them" (Genesis 37:8).

They hatched a plan to kill him, but ended up throwing

him in a pit and selling him into slavery. Eventually, he earned the favor of an Egyptian officer named Potiphar. He put Joseph in charge of everything he owned. But when Joseph resisted Potiphar's wife's advances, she lied about him and he was thrown into prison. Even in prison, Joseph wasn't forgotten: "But the Lord was with Joseph in the prison and showed him his faithful love. And the Lord made Joseph a favorite with the prison warden" (Gen. 39:21).

Eventually, through a series of divine events, Joseph was brought before Pharaoh to interpret a dream that was troubling him. It had been thirteen years since Joseph was thrown into that pit. He's not the same arrogant young man who taunted his brothers. "Then Pharaoh said to Joseph, 'I had a dream last night, and no one here can tell me what it means. But I have heard that when you hear about a dream you can interpret it.'…'It is beyond my power to do this,' Joseph replied. 'But God can tell you what it means and set you at ease'" (Gen. 41:15-16).

Joseph told the Pharaoh that a severe seven-year famine was coming to Egypt and the dream was a warning to prepare. Pharaoh needed to put someone in charge of gathering and storing food so the people wouldn't starve.

> So Pharaoh asked his officials, "Can we find anyone else like this man so obviously filled with the spirit of God?" Then Pharaoh said to Joseph, "Since God has revealed the meaning of the dreams to you, clearly no one else is as intelligent or wise as you are. You will be in charge of my

court, and all my people will take orders from you. Only I, sitting on my throne, will have a rank higher than yours" (Genesis 41:38-40).

Filled by the Spirit of God. Wise. Intelligent. Where did these qualities come from? I don't like the answer. You probably won't either. But those qualities were born from thirteen years of pain and suffering with no obvious explanation or good coming from them. Each trial was shaping and preparing Joseph's heart and character for God's ultimate plan: placing Joseph in a position where he saved millions of people from starvation and was reconciled to his family. It was then that he was able to say: "You intended to harm me, but God intended it all for good. He brought me to this position so I could save the lives of many people" (Gen. 50:20). I've heard it said that God is more interested in our character than our comfort. Joseph provides a powerful example of why.

It increases our gratefulness.

Can I be honest? When I hear people complain about stupid things, it irritates me. Sometimes it makes me angry. I guess God is still working on shaping my character. However, I'm sure you know what I mean. When we're confronting dark places and nursing deep wounds, we don't have much tolerance for whining about the superficial.

Pain and illness has made me incredibly grateful for things other people may take for granted. I'm beyond thankful for a pain-free day. I relish when I'm able to fully enjoy an outing with my family. More and more, I'm learning to be grateful for the deeper, sweeter relationship I have with God because of this long journey of suffering. He's showing me how to enjoy the moment and let Him worry about the future.

Recently, my son Micah went through a frightening stretch of out-of-control blood sugars related to his cystic fibrosis. This was unchartered territory for both of us. There was lots of researching the Internet, late night calls with doctors, and desperate prayers. Although his levels lowered just as it was time for a quarterly checkup with his pulmonologist. I was still concerned. Prolonged high blood sugars can negatively affect the entire body, including lung function and weight gain. His last two checkups had been worrisome. Although I prayed, I was prepared for another bad report from the doctor. Instead, she came into the room with a huge smile on her face. She said, "Micah, for six months I have been crying over your test results. But today I'm crying for a good reason! Your results are perfect!" His pulmonary function tests were the best they had been in eighteen months. He'd gained five pounds, after six months of losing weight.

This news was all the sweeter because of the struggle we had just been though. I thought, *There will be more battles ahead, but today is a good day*. I told the doctor it was the result of prayer. I reminded Micah this was God's doing. I thanked God the whole way home. "Yet I am confident I will see the LORD's goodness while I am here in the land of the living. Wait patiently for the LORD. Be brave and courageous. Yes, wait patiently for the LORD." (Psalm 27:13-14).

Just like the pain of childbirth gives way to a beautiful child, God can bring beautiful circumstances from pain. It is sometimes a long process. It has taken years for me to give birth to a chronic illness ministry at my church, a new turn in my online and writing ministry, an ever-deepening sense of compassion for others in pain, and most importantly, a sweeter relationship and dependence on God. As brutal as it may seem, we have to pay the price to recognize and appreciate the reward.

When we doubt that anyone understands our pain, when we don't see how any good can come from our suffering, remember our ultimate example of beauty in the brokenness. Jesus endured suffering and sacrifice beyond our comprehension. And it gave birth to the most beautiful redemption story ever told.

Hope That Heals

"In the same way I will not cause pain without allowing something new to be born," says the Lord.
Isaiah 66:9 (NCV)

My Invisible Wound... Shame
HOPE'S STORY

Who the world sees...

For years, my nickname was "Sunshine." It's amazing how we can compartmentalize our pain. Privately, I had long, incredibly dark years where my world was so horrible. Socially, however, I was always very outgoing and gregarious to compensate for my insecurities and deep wounds. I've always been a nurturer, trying to give other people what I've wanted so desperately myself.

What lies beneath the surface...

It's difficult for me to share parts of my story, not only because of the deep emotional wounds, but because I dissociated myself from some memories of my childhood. Over the years, my psyche has simply blocked certain time periods from my mind for my own survival and protection.

From the moment I was born, I was viewed as a pain to my family. I was a very large baby and my mother almost died giving birth to me. I was cared for by relatives while my mother recovered. I'm not sure exactly how long I was there, but it prevented the natural bonding that typically happens between mother and child during those first days and weeks of life. That traumatic start would foreshadow the instability and lack of connection and nurturing that would characterize much of my life.

My father always had a prominent role in the church, but behind closed doors he was an angry, brutal man. If one of us fell down and bled, my father would whip us for making a mess. Often, he would be calmly eating dinner and then suddenly fly into a fit of rage. Whoever happened to be sitting closest to him would bear the physical brunt of his irrational wrath. Once, my father tried to make me do something I couldn't do. I don't even remember what it was. What I do remember is that he was so terrifying that I passed out. I was just five years old. To this day, I feel incredibly panicked and trapped when people try to make me do something I can't do.

My mother was cold, detached, and offered us little protection—especially me. My sisters were pretty and petite. I was big boned. My hands were twice the size of theirs. I felt so incredibly ugly. The shame I felt about my identity was reinforced often. One time, I remember all of us girls getting dressed up to go somewhere special. My mother looked at me in disgust and said, "You are such an embarrassment." Shame is not about making mistakes. It's feeling you *are* a mistake. I believed everything about me was a mistake.

I grieved my lack of femininity. I wanted to look more like my sisters. When puberty hit, I became extremely busty. But instead of making me feel more confident, it made me feel even more uncomfortable about my appearance. It also opened the door for more abuse. My parents raised money for charities by standing outside businesses, asking for donations. Sometimes they would send me into bars to use my "assets" to get money from drunken men. I wasn't more than eleven or twelve years old. They were driven to raise money, not by compassion, but for the awards and recognition they would get from the community.

Invisible Wounds

When I wasn't being belittled, beaten or abused, I was simply ignored. It pains me to look at old pictures. I look so lost and neglected. In the midst of all this tragedy, I was molested by someone who stayed at our home and later by a family member. When I told my mother about these incidents, she didn't believe me. Because of the abuse and neglect, we moved often. My parents never wanted to stick around long enough for anyone to figure out what was going on. I never had friends. I never felt connected.

Somewhere in the midst of my tragic story, God was working in my heart. Despite the very faulty view of God and church that I received from my parents, I was a little evangelist. I would give "sermons" to my siblings. One of my brothers accepted Jesus at one of my "services."

By the time I was teenager, I was my father's favorite target. He blamed me for everything that had ever gone wrong in his life. One time, my father was about to whip me. For the first time, my mother stood up for me. A short time later, I moved out to live with an older sibling. I bounced from sibling to sibling.

Eventually, I ended up staying at a YWCA and started working for a sales company. The people I worked with turned out to be dangerous people. I knew I had to get away from them, but I didn't know where to go. About that time, my father called me. Incredibly, he said, "I have a very bad feeling about where you are and who you are with. Come home." Even in all his dysfunction, God used him to remove me from that danger. Still, I was scared to go home. My mother arranged for me to rent a room upstairs. For whatever reason, my father would not come up to my rented room. When he became violent, I could retreat upstairs. It was my safe place.

I began working at a hospital as a secretary. I was always very smart. However, intellect and excellence were never encouraged in my home. I see things differently than a lot of people, so I have often been rebuffed or misunderstood. I feel like my gifts have often been pushed aside as an irritant because they aren't packaged right. It has compounded my shame and disconnection. For years, I hid my intelligence behind humor or diminished it to earn others' validation or approval.

When my mom got sick when I was a young adult, I took care of her. She said, "Hope, you have a gift." I loved learning and started nursing school to earn my license. I eventually got my master's degree.

During this time, I married a Christian man who loved God. However, because of his own childhood brokenness, he was often cold and distant. My marriage became another wound and another source of shame.

When my healing began...

Home, school and marriage all had pain and shame attached to them. My work became both my escape and a conduit to my healing. I was working at a religious healthcare facility that encouraged employees to go to seminary. Because of my background, I was so wounded and desperate. My view of God was difficult to separate from my experiences with my parents. The hospital offered to pay for me to go. I jumped at the chance. I had never been in that kind of loving, supportive atmosphere before. I received counseling and group therapy as part of my training. I was surrounded by people full of love and grace who invested in me. I began to discover who God really is.

A pivotal moment was when God spoke to me through 1 John 2:1-2: "My dear children, I am writing this to you so that you will not sin. But if anyone does sin, we have an advocate who pleads our case before the Father. He is Jesus Christ, the one who is truly righteous. He himself is the sacrifice that atones for our sins—and not only our sins but the sins of all the world."

I realized that the Holy Spirit is my advocate—my defense lawyer! When anyone wants to attack me or who I am, they have to go to the cross. The cross has released me from all my guilt and shame. I had always believed that there was something bad or wrong with me that couldn't be fixed. That day I realized that there was nothing in me that God couldn't fix. For the first time, I truly trusted that I could go to God with anything. I didn't have to be ashamed. Gradually, He has helped me to quit chasing others' approval and rest in His unwavering opinion of me.

My marriage was never easy until the day my husband died. I prayed about it often and stayed because I believe God assured me He would give me the grace to do so and would work through my obedience. God challenged me to love my husband without expectation. I began to go out of my way to show him acts of love. I changed the way I spoke to him. It transformed the atmosphere in our home. He slowly began to reciprocate with kind words. It remained a difficult journey, but it brought life into the desert of our relationship. He eventually sought and found a measure of healing for his own wounds. Parts of our relationship remained painful and highly imperfect, but we developed a partnership built on our mutual spiritual foundation. He was supportive of my career and leadership ambitions. We rooted for each other. A beautiful sweetness developed between us.

Today, I still struggle with those old triggers. Shame wants to envelop me regularly. I fight depression. But I'm still here. I'm not alone. God has given me beautiful friends to walk alongside me through the dark days that sometimes still come. I have a blessed life.

Some might look at my story and say, "Where was God?" I look back and see God's hand on my life at every turn. He has never left me.

How God is using my pain...

I have always served from that place of pain and shame. I'm open to other people's stories and want to help them see God in the midst of it. I have the ability to help women recognize the lessons, emotions and pain of the people in the Bible, and apply them to their own stories. God used my story over and over again in my role as nurse and caregiver. I've been in leadership roles in healing and recovery ministries and have used my gift of teaching often. Because of my own background, I have been an effective advocate for others who have been abused. Wherever I've worked or served, people still remember me years later and have incredibly glowing things to say about me. This is not because of me. I could never see these things in myself at the time. It is only because every interaction I have with others is empowered by the love, healing and grace God has given me.

CHAPTER 7

The Power Of Telling Our Stories

Are you in the dark just now in your circumstances, or
in your life with God?…When you are in the dark, listen,
and God will give you a very precious message for
someone else when you get into the light.
~ Oswald Chambers

One of the biggest needs we have as humans is to feel understood. There's nothing quite like the feeling of sharing our hearts, fears, and pain with someone who gets us. A kindred spirit. A soul sister. Those kinds of bonds energize and empower us.

I believe that's why the enemy works so relentlessly to keep us quiet. To convince us that *no one* could possibly understand our struggles, our mistakes, our anxieties. And beyond that, that no one would even particularly *care*. After all, everyone has his or her own problems. We *look* fine. Who would really *believe* us? For those and other reasons, I suffered in silence. I finally shared about my chronic pain battle—and the emotional and spiritual struggles that stemmed from it—

when I made this decision: My pain is not going to be wasted. I have to know something good is coming to come from this. I have to know God is going to use this to help someone else. I had no idea what a huge role it would play in my own healing.

As my pain intensified over these last couple of years, my coping mechanisms failed me. My physical strength was waning. My emotional reserves were dangerously low. One night, I got *angry*. I knew God had a purpose in my pain—*but I didn't really care*. I knew He was using it to build my character and depth of compassion—*but I just wanted to be healed*. I was tired of feeling miserable. I was weary of feeling alone.

Then, I clearly heard this in my spirit: "Share it."

I put up a fight. No one is going to get this. It will be embarrassing. How do I share it? Who do I share it with? Then the thought came to me about a new website I had just heard about called The Mighty *(themighty.com)*, dedicated to stories of people who struggle with chronic illness—either personally or as a parent of a child with a disease or disability. Within the space of about an hour, I dug deep to share my journey and how God was using it in my life for good. I wasn't ready to talk about it publicly, but maybe I could write about it—if for no other reason but to remind myself of God's activity in the midst of my misery. Maybe in the process, someone else could relate to my struggles. Pouring it out on the page, for the very first time, felt simultaneously frightening and freeing.

The next morning, my heart pounding, I emailed it to the editor. She emailed me back with lightning speed: *Hi Melinda, I'm so thrilled to have you on The Mighty. I've been working to get more posts about invisible illnesses. Thank you for this piece. It's great.*

The article, "What My Invisible Disease Gave Me Eyes to See," was up on the website before the end of the day. Messages and comments started pouring in from others who were also in the shadows, living with silent pain—physical, spiritual, or emotional. They got it. Many shared their stories, doubts, and struggles, as well.

Revelation 12:11 tells us that our testimony—our story—is one of two things that defeats the enemy: "And they have defeated him by the blood of the Lamb and by their testimony. And they did not love their lives so much that they were afraid to die." It shatters the loneliness and defeat of isolation. We feel hopeful and empowered. It inspires and empowers others. It makes it safe for others to share their stories and express their doubts, fears, and discouragement. We then have the opportunity to encourage, pray, and speak truth into each other's lives. *That* is what Satan fears.

Time to Drop the Cloak of Invisibility

Often, we walk around in pain and despair, safely covered by our cloaks of invisibility. We feel sorry for ourselves. We think no one understands. Pain is a cruel master that tends to demand self-focus. But how can others understand if we don't tell them? How can they support us, pray for us, and love on us if we don't give them the opportunity?

God made us for community. We weren't meant to go through difficulties alone. In Galatians 6:2, it says, "Share each other's burdens, and in this way obey the law of Christ." Notice it doesn't say, "Find someone to bear your burdens." It says, "share *each other's* burdens" (emphasis mine). God works through others to encourage and heal us, but He also wants to work through us, even in our brokenness (maybe especially in our brokenness!) to heal others.

The second part of that verse says, "in this way obey the law of Christ." The law it refers to is in John 13:34-35: "So now I am giving you a new commandment: Love each other. Just as I have loved you, you should love each other. Your love for one another will prove to the world that you are my disciples."[1]

One of the most loving acts someone can do for me in my pain is to pray for me. It's the most powerful, loving act we can do for someone else. It requires vulnerability, particularly when we're in a place of dark discouragement. We have to be honest and real about our doubts and difficulties. We can't sugarcoat it. When people have asked what they could do for me, sometimes I've simply said, "Pray for me. Because I'm struggling to pray for myself right now." Or, "I'm having a really rough week. I'm in pain and I'm discouraged. Please pray." There's an urgency in those kinds of requests that helps people understand the depth of your need.

There is power in your pain. Go tell your story.

God wants us to speak truth and perspective into each other's lives. Recently, I had a terribly discouraging week. I had challenging things going on in nearly every area of my life. My health was stinky. Overall, I felt I was ineffective, a disappointment to God and a big, fat failure. I don't go there as often as I used to, but when I do, it isn't pretty.

And then I went to church. The place where we all think we're supposed to act happy. A couple of younger women I happen to adore came up to me and asked, "How are you?" I'm supposed to be the older, wiser woman who shows them how it's done, right? Maybe so. But I told them anyway. I mean I really told them. Not all the details, but I conveyed the depth of my discouragement.

One of them immediately said, "You know that's not true, right? You are not ineffective. You are not a disappointment. God is enabling you to do some awesome things." She wasn't just being nice. My friend *is* kind, but she's also a bold truth teller. She was speaking truth into my weary soul. She was giving me some much-needed perspective.

At my chronic illness group, there is a rare level of authenticity and sharing. We pray for each other. I mean *really* pray for each other. Deep, desperate, Spirit-filled prayers. These are the kind of women we have to seek out. These are the women God wants us to be to others. Bold truth tellers. Real, godly, drop-to-our-knees prayer warriors. Women who will go to God in prayer regularly and specifically.

Find Your Inner Circle

Vulnerability is risky. Not everyone *will* understand our pain. If they haven't gone through it, they can't relate. They might say we need stronger faith. They may not understand that healing from grief, pain, or loss is not a linear process. Most people know what to do to help in crisis, but long-term wounds make people uncomfortable. They can't fix it. We have to let go of unrealistic expectations, ladies. We have to let people off the hook. For the most part, people don't mean to say the wrong things. The benefit of reaching out—for you and for others—is worth the risk.

Invisible Wounds

Don't hesitate to share your story as God leads you. However, seek out a trusted few with whom to share your deepest emotions. I think of Jesus. He shared the testimony God had given Him with the masses, but He shared much more deeply and intimately with the twelve disciples. Even among them, His closest confidantes were reduced to just three, His inner circle: Peter, James and John. Ask God to bring kind, wise, supportive people into your life. Pray for discernment. Then take the risk to reach out to them. Share each other's burdens. **Here are a few qualities to look for:**

THEY'RE "ME TOO" PEOPLE. That's what my pastor calls them. How do you find them? If you sense a connection with someone who seems compassionate and real, share a bit of your struggle. If they hear your heart and respond with "me too" and are vulnerable in sharing their own battles, they're a keeper.

THEY KNOW WHEN TO BE QUIET. In his book, *The View from a Hearse*, Joe Bayly writes about how two men came to comfort him in his deep grief after the death of his three young sons. The first one talked constantly, assuring Joe he'd see them again one day and attempting to explain why it happened and how God works. Joe writes that he knew the man said things that were true, but he was unmoved by his words.

The second man spoke little. He "didn't talk. He didn't ask leading questions. He just sat beside me for an hour or more, listened when I said something, answered briefly, prayed simply, left."[2] Joe writes that though both men had good intentions, he wanted the first man to leave, but was sad to see the second man go.

Sometimes God will bring "second men" (or women) into our lives when we least expect it. For a period of months, I traveled weekly to a health clinic a couple of hours from my home. A friend called me one day and said, 'I'm going with you next time. I'm not taking no for an answer.' Honestly, I didn't want her to go. It was a sweet gesture, but I felt too emotionally fragile to make conversation. I was too weary to put on a happy face. But I knew this friend well enough to know that she really *wouldn't* take no for an answer.

When I arrived at her house to pick her up, she ran up to my window and said, "I'm so sorry. I realized I have an appointment today. But I called Sue and asked her to come with you instead. I really don't want you to be alone."

Sue goes to my church. Sue is a wonderful person, but I didn't really know her that well. Making small talk with a friend seemed overwhelming. Making conversation with someone I didn't really know was more than I could take. I couldn't hold back the tears any longer.

With a sweet smile, Sue got into the car. As I began to drive, we were both silent. Finally she said in the kindest, most sincere way possible, "Melinda, I want you to know that you don't have to talk. You don't have to make conversation with me. I'm not here for you to entertain me. I'm here to support you and pray for you." And she meant it. A bond formed between us that day. On a couple of other occasions, I invited Sue to go with me. She has become a sweet source of prayer support and encouragement to me.

Invisible Wounds

THEY KNOW GREAT PAIN BUT ARE BETTER—INSTEAD OF BITTER—FOR IT. There's a woman at my church who I'm honored to call friend. She absolutely radiates Jesus. You would never guess her difficult and painful past of abuse and broken relationships.

Another amazing woman that God put into my life has been through a horrific history of sexual and emotional abuse and abandonment by her father. She has an ongoing battle with depression, but it does not define her.

My friend Lori has been waging an exhausting battle with AML leukemia over the last four years. She has had multiple courses of chemotherapy that nearly killed her and ultimately a bone marrow transplant. Yet, she clings tenaciously to what she knows to be true about God.

These women know pain. They are real about their struggles and doubts, but battle every day to claim joy, hope, and victory. They exude the power and peace of Jesus as they rise above their circumstances. These women inspire and encourage me. They don't judge my doubts and feelings. They pray for me often, and I do the same for them. Because of their hard-won credibility and wisdom, they are able to speak truth into my life and experiences in ways others couldn't.

I used to think strength meant suffering silently. I believed the most powerful testimony was delivered *after* the painful, difficult circumstance had passed. When we're on the other side of the darkness. But what I'm realizing is that our testimony is perhaps the most powerful when we can't see much daylight, but still reach out to others and choose—moment-by-moment—to cling to the truth of God's Word and believe in His goodness. God uses it to heal us. He uses it heal others.

Come out of the shadows, friend. It's time to drop the cloak of invisibility.

Let's bear each other's burdens. There is power in your pain, mighty warrior. Go tell your story.

❋

Hope That Heals

"My mouth will tell of your righteous deeds, of your saving acts all day long— though I know not how to relate them all. I will come and proclaim your mighty acts, Sovereign LORD; I will proclaim your righteous deeds, yours alone."
Psalm 71:15-16 (NIV)

My Invisible Wound... Secrets
KATIE'S STORY

What the world sees...

People think I'm very happy. They assume that my whole life has been a pretty charmed middle-class existence. They perceive me as a well adjusted and accomplished risk taker, a brave person with a really good life.

What lies beneath the surface...

For most of my life, I've been a secret keeper. Starting at the tender age of three, I was molested. The abuse continued for several years. Like so many victims, I didn't feel like I could tell anyone. I was so ashamed. I had so much fear. My fractured little mind tried to forget. It was safest to keep quiet. It's been said that our secrets make us sick. I'm living proof of that.

Secrets are intimate. With sexual abuse, a memory is created that only you and the abuser share. A disgusting intimacy exists between the two of you. Abusers prey on a child's vulnerability in so many ways. My abuser would say, "Don't tell. It's our little secret." Or sometimes he would threaten, "You better not tell!" He made me feel shameful, as though I was consenting to his acts, when what I really wanted to do was run far, far away.

I wanted to tell my father. I was daddy's little girl. If anyone could help me, Daddy could. But my father battled alcoholism. Although he was never aggressive toward me, he became violent when he drank. I thought that if he ever knew what happened to me, he would kill my abuser and I'd lose my family and everyone who brought me security. So, I didn't tell him or anyone else.

To handle the pain, I buried those memories so deep inside me that even I couldn't retrieve them. But I couldn't shake the feeling of shame and self-loathing that pervaded my every thought and deed. I also had another little secret: my battle with lust. You might think that the trauma of sexual abuse would keep you from those kinds of desires. Often, it's just the opposite. When I think back to my childhood, all the way back to my earliest memories as a wee little girl, I can't ever remember not knowing about sexual things. This made me feel so different from my friends. I lived in a prison of isolation that no one could see.

By the time I was a teenager, the self-loathing was so deep and dark that I believed the only way out of my pain was suicide. As I began contemplating suicide, my best friend's mom started going to church and praying for her daughter and her daughter's friends. I truly believe my salvation at the age of sixteen was a direct answer to her prayers. Now I knew Jesus, but still no one knew my secrets.

Once I became a Christian, I got along pretty well until my senior year of college. One day I read a magazine article about sexual abuse and I got really upset, disgusted, angry. I couldn't understand my feelings or why the article was affecting me so deeply. I asked God to show me why I was responding this way. One by one, the memories of sexual abuse returned. I felt physically ill and sobbed for days. For the first time in my life, I told someone my secret. My best friend listened and held me and walked with me down that painful memory lane.

Invisible Wounds

My healing was far from over. A few months later I started dating a Christian man who I thought was the man of my dreams. Within a year we were talking about marriage. Then one day, out of the blue, he announced that it was over. My heart was shattered and my struggle with self-worth raged again. I stopped eating, wasting away to a mere seventy-eight pounds. It was a perilous time. Had it not been for my roommates, my mom, and the help of a great counselor, I don't think I would have made it through the pain.

When my healing began...

Eventually, I moved to a new area for a fresh start and this is where healing really took place. For a full year, I committed to doing nothing but getting to know God better and allowing Him to heal my heart. I lived alone. I didn't date. I did nothing but go to work, go to church, and spend time studying my Bible and praying. I was in therapy with God and it was a time of both purification and preparation. It was during this time that I really got to know God and His unconditional love for me. Little by little, I learned to trust my heavenly Father. At the end of that year, I met my husband. God gave me a wonderful man, a man who really loved me, a man I could trust with my secrets!

All these years, I thought that I was alone in this terrible, disgusting intimacy with my abuser—that the secret was just between us. God revealed to me that it was not just between my abuser and me. *He* was there. He knew every detail of what happened and every emotion I felt. He had always known my secret. You might think, "If God was there, why didn't He do something?" We all have free will. We live in a fallen world. That means men like my abuser sometimes make terrible choices to hurt children. I don't know all the reasons why it happened, but I do know that God didn't abandon me. That is what matters most to me. I was not alone. God showed me that He would never leave me and that there was nothing I couldn't share with Him.

I knew my healing was complete when decades later I encountered my abuser at a party. He was not the same man I knew as a child. Because of many poor choices, he was a shell of his former self. Physically, he was disabled and broken. As I looked at him, God impressed upon my heart to take him a plate of food and serve him. I couldn't believe it. It was as if God was saying, "When you were vulnerable as a child, he took advantage of you. He didn't show you kindness. Now he's vulnerable. I want you to do for him what he didn't do for you. Show him what it means to serve." As I handed him that plate of food and looked into his eyes, I knew I was free. I had forgiven him and he no longer had a hold on me. God had restored me.

I never planned to share my story publicly. As far as I was concerned it was over and done and I could forget about it. But God had other ideas. We were on a family vacation when I woke up in the middle of the night with the distinct impression that I needed to tell my story to my son who had recently graduated from college. This seemed odd so I prayed, "Lord, if you want me to tell him, give me some alone time with him tomorrow." The next day we found ourselves on a long walk, just the two of us. As I shared my long-held secret with my son, I was shocked by his reply: "Mom, do you know how many girls I met at college who have experienced abuse? But they don't know you can heal and get through it. You have to tell them, Mom. You have to share your story!"

How God is using my pain...

My abuser took so many things from me. But he gave me one gift: compassion for the hurting. Over the last year, I've shared my secret with my pastor and his wife. They gave me the opportunity to share my story with the women of my church. Now God is asking me to share it with an even wider audience. Every day, I believe God is showing me new ways to use my story to help others find the freedom I've found. Keeping secrets made me sick. Telling my secret is bringing a new layer of healing and giving hope to others who need to be made well.

Next Steps

I pray that this book has brought you a measure of healing and encouragement. However, as we well know, healing can be a long, ongoing process. It is one that God works out in us, perhaps throughout our entire lives. Some wounds may not completely heal this side of heaven. More and more, I look forward to the day when all the pain and suffering in this broken world is over. The day that our Creator makes all things right.

Until then, our only hope is to trust the Healer. While the heading says "Next Steps," I can't tell you what *your* next step should be. Only God completely knows your broken places and where you need to go next. I believe without a doubt that as you continue to seek His guidance and follow His leading, step-by-step, He will comfort and mend your hurting heart and show His strength and provision in your circumstances in ways you couldn't have possibly imagined. He has done that for me in ways I can't adequately describe.

Invisible Wounds

I LOVINGLY CHALLENGE YOU TO PRAYERFULLY CONSIDER THESE QUESTIONS:

❀ How have I sensed God speaking to me as I've read this book?

❀ Is there bitterness or resentment in my heart toward God or someone in my life who has wounded me? How can I move toward letting go of that?

❀ Am I suffering silently? Who is at least one person I can reach out to as a source of prayer and support?

❀ What is the next step I believe God is leading me to take in my healing or difficult circumstances?

You may not know the answers to some of these questions. That's okay. *God does.* Your only responsibility is to come to Him. Humbly. Broken. Psalm 34:18 tells us, "The Lord is close to the brokenhearted; he rescues those whose spirits are crushed." When you seek Him for wisdom in your situation, He *will* provide it. He promises: "If you need wisdom, ask our generous God, and he will give it to you. He will not rebuke you for asking." (James 1:5)

The way God works in each of our hearts and lives is so unique and beautifully different. However, I will share with you a few steps and resources that God used powerfully in my own healing process:

❀ **SUPPORT GROUPS.** Once I began to share more openly, I received an incredible outpouring of love and support from my couples' small group at my church and from my chronic illness group. Even women I don't know well who heard my story when I gave it

100

publicly at the conference still come up to me months later and ask how I'm doing. Some assure me that they continue to pray for me often. You'll find a Discussion Guide in this book that you can use to go through this book with a friend or a small group.

PRAYER JOURNALING. Maybe it's just because I'm a writer, but I love to journal my prayers. I've done it for years. It's been especially freeing over this last year. I think it's because when I put it down on paper, I feel a release. I've written my letter to God for the day and can more easily leave those burdens with Him. I can also look back and see His provision and faithfulness right there in black and white. At times, it has brought me to tears to realize the personal depth of His love and care for me.

DIGGING DEEP INTO HIS WORD. As I wrote this book, I poured over Scripture, resources and commentaries. God opened my eyes to new lessons, comfort and applications, even in stories that I've heard since I was a tiny girl in Sunday School. He met me there in the pages of His Word so personally and so sweetly. He assured me time and time again that He sees me, He loves me and I can trust Him. That has been the biggest factor in my ability to walk through the very painful, discouraging days that continue to be a part of my reality. Dig deep, ladies. He'll meet you there.

STUDIES. There are two studies I wanted to highlight that were absolutely pivotal in the transforming work God did in my heart. He used these studies to speak right to my weary soul. I know God may use other resources to speak to you in your unique situation, but these are definitely worth checking out:

- *Stronger: Finding Hope in Fragile Places* by Angela Thomas
- *The Storm Inside Study Guide: Trade The Chaos Of How You Feel For The Truth Of Who You Are* by Sheila Walsh (Sheila also has a trade book of the same name.)

COUNSELING. Sharing and processing my struggles and wounds (not just the ones shared in this book) with godly Christian counselors has been a significant part of my healing process. If you don't know of a counselor or who to ask for a recommendation, the American Association of Christian Counselors *(aacc.net)* is a good place to start. Under the "Resources" menu on their website, you can search for a counselor in your area *(http://www.aacc.net/resources/find-a-counselor)*.

SHARE YOUR STORY. Another "Next Step" for you may be to tell your story. No one except God can tell you when and how to do that. Pray and ask Him to show you. In His timing, He will. I'd be honored to be a vehicle for you to do that. If you're interested in being a guest writer on my blog's "Share Your Story" feature, please see my website for guidelines *(melindameans.com/contact-us/share-your-story-guidelines)*.

Discussion Guide

——✳——✳——✳——✳——

Dear Healing Woman,

I know that I've tackled a lot of difficult issues in these pages. My prayer is that by the time you read this, God has begun to heal those broken places (maybe even ones you didn't know you had) in your heart and mind. As we well know, healing is a journey.

In order to help you process what you've been reading and learning, I'm including this Discussion Guide. You can certainly go through these questions by yourself. But here's the thing: *I don't want you to be alone anymore.* For that reason, I highly encourage you to go through these questions in a small group. *Maybe you could even choose just one friend and go through the book and this Guide together.* Remember that God uses community as part of our healing. It was and is a huge part of mine. It's written so that you can work through the book together in six weeks/sessions, although you can combine chapters if you'd like to work through it in a shorter time frame.

Invisible Wounds

You'll find a "Survival Kit" on my website that includes a prayer journal, Scripture verse printables and a playlist of songs for encouragement during difficult times *(melindameans.com/survival-kit)*. These are designed to enhance your personal and group time with God.

You'll find questions and a verse to memorize for each session. Because I found it so difficult to pray at times during my journey, I'm including a prayer at the end of each session. I also found it helpful to read the Psalms and use those as my prayers. You'll notice I haven't given you any "Action Steps" to take each week. Instead, I simply encourage you to ask for and follow the Holy Spirit's leading. He never fails.

Your wounds are *not* invisible to God, my friend. I pray this book and this Guide will lead you closer to the Hope that Heals.

Love, Melinda

CHAPTER ONE: THE PAIN THAT NO ONE SEES

Hope that Heals:

I have cared for you since you were born. Yes, I carried you before you were born. I will be your God throughout your lifetime—until your hair is white with age. I made you, and I will care for you. I will carry you along and save you.
Isaiah 46:3-4

Read Dear Hurting Woman, Foreword and Chapter One

1. We all have hidden pain—hurts so deep and raw that we don't feel safe to express them. When you look in the mirror, what do you see? How do you think God sees you?

2. What are some reasons that you haven't shared your hurts, disappointments and doubts about God with others?

3. What are some ways hiding your pain has cost you?

4. In this chapter, I write, "When our joy, freedom and hope rest on an outcome, instead of a Person, we will ultimately be disappointed." Even when we receive the outcome we've longed for, it can disappoint us. Why do you think that's the case? Give an example of an outcome you received that didn't give you the payoff you imagined it would.

5. "Do not be afraid, for I have ransomed you. I have called you by name; you are mine. When you go

through deep waters, I will be with you. When you go through rivers of difficulty, you will not drown. When you walk through the fire of oppression, you will not be burned up; the flames will not consume you. For I am the Lord, your God, the Holy One of Israel, your Savior." (Isaiah 43:1-3) As you read this verse, what does it mean to you to know that God has called you by name, that you are His?

6. Looking back, think of a specific example of how God was walking through the "fire of oppression" or the "rivers of difficulty" with you, even though you may not have recognized it at the time.

7. In Rachel's story, she talked about how she was a slave to her cravings for alcohol. What cravings have you in bondage? How are you using those things to replace a hunger only God can fill?

Dear Father, Help me to see myself as You see me—valuable, loved and beautiful. I want to believe that You see me in my suffering. Make Yourself real to me. Help me to recognize Your presence and activity in the midst of my pain and doubts. Amen.

CHAPTER TWO: IS GOD REALLY GOOD?

Hope that Heals:
Taste and see that the Lord is good;
blessed is the one who takes refuge in him.
Psalm 34:8 (NIV)

Read Chapter Two and Lindsey's Story

1. What circumstances or events in your life (either past or present) have caused you to question God's goodness?

2. As you read this book, did God reveal any lies that you believe about Him? What are they? Ask Him to help you replace them with Truth.

3. "His delay (in ending suffering) is because He is merciful, not because He is callous or indifferent." What do you think about that statement? How does it change your perspective about God's goodness?

4. Our American culture tells us that we "deserve" to be happy, that we should always have what we want. How have you bought into that mindset? How has it affected your relationship or attitude toward God? After reading this chapter, has your view of the fairness of suffering changed? How?

5. God made the choice to send His only Son to die for us. Jesus came to earth to endure unimaginable suffering so we could have eternal life in heaven. They didn't have to do this. It was motivated by their great

love for us. Yet, it's often so difficult for us to trust God's love and goodness. What specifically makes it difficult for you to trust God's love and that He's working for your good?

6. Share or think about a time that God met you powerfully and sweetly in your suffering. Thank Him for that right now.

7. In Lindsey's story, she shares how she was so focused on her pain and loss, she couldn't fully enjoy the blessings right in front of her. Can you relate? If so, how? Ask God to show you how to recognize and appreciate His gifts more fully.

Dear Father, You are good. You are worthy of all my trust. That truth is not changed by my fears and doubts. You are bigger than all the barriers that I have put up in my heart that keep me from intimate relationship with You. Reveal the lies that I have been believing about You. Help me to trust You more. Amen.

CHAPTER THREE: THE HARD ROAD THAT LEADS TO HOPE

Hope that Heals:
Don't be afraid, for I am with you.
Don't be discouraged, for I am your God.
I will strengthen you and help you.
I will hold you up with my victorious right hand.
Isaiah 41:10

Read Chapter Three and Barb's Story

1. We often feel guilty or disrespectful when we are angry with God. We hesitate to share our true thoughts with Him, even though He already knows every one! How might it help your healing to be able to go to God with your anger and frustration?

2. Prayer is often the most difficult when we need it the most. Remember, even saying the name "Jesus!" in the midst of our despair is a prayer! There is so much power in just saying His name. Why do you think it's so hard to pray when we're feeling the most vulnerable and in need of His strength? Who is one person you could ask to pray for you when you feel overwhelmed and unable to pray for yourself?

3. Unending pain and uncertain circumstances cause us to fear for the future. How has fear held you back from healing and depending on God?

4. We all like to feel in control. Even when we're certain

we are, we're deceived. Control is an illusion. How have you been like Jacob—trying to heal your pain and/or solve your problems on your own strength?

5. Feeling like we need to "perform" is a battle for so many of us! Why do we feel like we need to perform? What is at the root of that for you? If you're not sure, ask God to reveal it to you.

6. Think of a time when you were especially aware of God's power in your life and circumstances. 2 Corinthians 12:9 says, "My grace is enough for you. When you are weak, my power is made perfect in you." (NCV) What can you do to be more conscious of tapping into His power and presence moment by moment?

7. In Barb's story, she shares transparently about her feelings of rejection and betrayal. Who has rejected or betrayed you that you feel bitterness toward? How do you think this is a barrier to your healing process?

Dear Father, My human nature wants comfort. I don't want to take the hard road. Yet I know that is where You want to meet me most sweetly. You are trustworthy. You are my only hope. Give me Your power to let go of trying to control my circumstances and trust You to give me what I need. I can't do it on my own. Amen.

CHAPTER FOUR: THE GOD WHO SEES ME

Hope that Heals:
Answer me, Lord, out of the goodness of your love;
in your great mercy turn to me.
Psalm 69:16

Read Chapter Four and Grace's Story

1. How does it make you feel to know that God sees every part of us—every hurt, thought and desire? Is it comforting, scary, overwhelming?

2. Hagar felt hopeless and forgotten as she wandered in the wilderness. Share a time that you felt forgotten by God. How did He reassure you of His presence and activity in your circumstances?

3. The angel of the Lord called Gideon "mighty warrior" before He fought a single battle! Isaiah 40:29 tells us: "He gives power to the weak and strength to the powerless." What thoughts and attitudes keep you from being the warrior God sees in you? Identify at least one Scripture verse that can help you combat those lies. If you don't know where to start, look to the verses at the end of this guide.

4. The woman with the issue of bleeding thought her biggest need was healing of her physical ailment. In fact, she most needed healing from her shame. She needed a Savior that could heal the deepest wounds

in her. What is your deepest need? Do not feel pressured to share this in a group if you don't feel comfortable or ready. God knows, my friend.

5.   Have you ever believed that God was completely absent when you needed Him the most desperately? Maybe that time is right now. Sometimes when we're in pain our perspective is clouded. God often uses other people to help us see His activity in our lives when we can't. If you feel comfortable, share with the group. If not, who is one person you can be vulnerable with who could help you recognize ways that God is present in your situation.

6.   Look back at Grace's story. Discuss the ways that God was present in Grace's broken life and circumstances even as she couldn't see or feel Him.

Dear Father, I'm so often like Hagar. I want to run from my circumstances. I want to run from You. I sometimes think You have forgotten me. Please help me to recognize Your love and presence even in the midst of circumstances I wouldn't have chosen. Help me to cling to the truth that You do see me. Amen.

CHAPTER FIVE: EMBRACING THE RACE WE'VE BEEN GIVEN

Hope that Heals:
We can make our plans, but the Lord determines our steps.
Proverbs 16:9

Read Chapter Five and Hannah's Story

1. When we're in pain, we tend to want someone else's life or circumstances. How has comparison and complaining affected your attitude toward your life and toward God?

2. Dr. Benjamin T. Mast has a powerful quote in his book, *Second Forgetting*, (referenced in this chapter). Discuss the concept of grumbling vs. groaning. How does it affect your mindset to know that God welcomes groaning?

3. Even Jesus—fully God and fully human—wanted deliverance from His pain. Yet He wanted God's will and plan more. For that reason, He walked a difficult path willingly. Where are you right now on the journey of acceptance of God's current plan for your life?

4. In 2 Corinthians 12:7, Paul had a "thorn" that God did not remove. We often see our "thorns" as handicaps. In what ways do you think Paul's ministry was enhanced because of this thorn?

Invisible Wounds

5. As we walk difficult paths, the way ahead seems foggy. Often, we can't see the next step in front of us. We're afraid to move forward. What next step in your journey are you afraid to take? Who can pray for you?

6. In Hannah's story, she talks about how she had her whole life planned out. Slowly, one by one, her plans were shattered. She says she began to choose to do those things that would help her move forward as she navigated this new, uncertain future (Bible study, engaging with community, etc.). What is at least one healthy step you can commit to taking this week? It may be simply having coffee with a friend.

Dear Father, You tell us in Your Word that Your plans are always good. Honestly, Your plans don't always seem good. I struggle at times to understand why You won't deliver me from this difficult race I'm running. Help me to trust You. Give me the power and courage to take the next step in my journey, even when I don't think I can. Remind me that You are already ahead of me. Amen.

CHAPTERS SIX AND SEVEN:
BEAUTY IN OUR BROKENNESS &
THE POWER OF TELLING OUR STORIES

Hope that Heals:

*What joy for those whose strength comes from
the Lord...When they walk through the Valley of
Weeping, it will become a place of refreshing springs.
The autumn rains will clothe it with blessings.*

Psalm 84:5-6

Read Chapters Six & Seven and Hope and Katie's Story

1. God wants to us our pain. He wants so much to bring beauty from our broken stories. Share a time where you saw God bring something unexpectedly beautiful from your pain.

2. Do you believe that pain can lead us to our destinies—to roles, jobs or ministries that we would never have considered or been equipped for without it? How have you seen this to be true in your own life?

3. God gave Joseph wonderful dreams about his future. But Joseph wasn't ready. God had to prepare him. Little did Joseph know that preparation would involve complete separation from his family, slavery and prison. Yet all those things prepared him for those dreams God gave him. In what ways can you see God using your pain to shape your character like He did Joseph's?

4. How have your struggles made you more grateful? What things or people are you more grateful for because of the difficulties you've faced?

5. Shame and fear of rejection often keep us quiet in our pain and struggles. What has or is keeping your from sharing your story with others?

6. Galatians 6:2 says, "Share each other's burdens, and in this way obey the law of Christ." Think of someone you know who is struggling. How can you reach out to that person this week?

7. Jesus had a trusted inner circle. Do you? Who is someone you know that exhibits the qualities of safe people outlined in this chapter? If God leads, what step can you take to share with or get to know that person better? If you can't think of anyone, pray that God would bring someone into your life with whom you can share safely.

8. Hope's Story is incredibly heartbreaking. Yet she is a beautiful, joyful woman. She still has significant struggles, but she knows that God has never left her. Discuss the ways that you can see God's intervention in the midst of Hope's tragedy.

9. When Katie began to share her secret, freedom and healing began. What secrets are making you sick? Like Katie, you may find that counseling is a necessary part of your journey before you are able to share those dark places with others. Take some time this week to consider if that is part of your healing journey. If you

don't know of a Christian counselor in your area, visit the American Association of Christian Counselors website *(aacc.net)*. Under the "Resources" tab, you can search for Christian counselors near you. Pray that God will lead you.

Dear Father, I love that You can bring beauty out of all the broken pieces of my life. I pray You will help me see how You are using my struggles to shape me. I know You want me to share my story with others as You lead me—for my good and for others.' Help me know who to share it with it, as well as when and how. Amen.

Hope that Heals
MORE VERSES FOR WHEN YOU'RE HURTING

A beautiful team of healing women helped me get out the message of *Invisible Wounds*. Most of the verses below are ones that they suggested I share with you in this section of the book. These Scriptures are ones they cling to in their darkest moments. These words are what encourage their weary hearts when they feel they can't take another step on their painful, often uncertain paths. I hope they encourage yours as well.

Psalm 16:8
I know the Lord is always with me. I will not be shaken, for he is right beside me.

Lamentations 3:22-24
The faithful love of the Lord never ends! His mercies never cease. Great is his faithfulness; his mercies begin afresh each morning. I say to myself, "The Lord is my inheritance; therefore, I will hope in him!"

Invisible Wounds

Psalm 103:2-5

Let all that I am praise the Lord; may I never forget the good things he does for me. He forgives all my sins and heals all my diseases. He redeems me from death and crowns me with love and tender mercies. He fills my life with good things. My youth is renewed like the eagle's!

Isaiah 40:29

He gives power to the weak and strength to the powerless.

Philippians 4:13

For I can do everything through Christ, who gives me strength.

Psalm 46:1

God is our refuge and strength, always ready to help in times of trouble.

2 Corinthians 12:9

My grace is all you need. My power works best in weakness.

Isaiah 43:19

For I am about to do something new. See, I have already begun! Do you not see it? I will make a pathway through the wilderness. I will create rivers in the dry wasteland.

Psalm 73:26

My health may fail, and my spirit may grow weak, but God remains the strength of my heart; he is mine forever.

Romans 5:3-5

We can rejoice, too, when we run into problems and trials, for we know that they help us develop endurance. And endurance develops strength of character, and character strengthens our confident hope of salvation. And this hope will not lead to disappointment. For we know how dearly God loves us, because he has given us the Holy Spirit to fill our hearts with his love.

Psalm 27:13-14

Yet I am confident I will see the Lord's goodness while I am here in the land of the living. Wait patiently for the Lord. Be brave and courageous. Yes, wait patiently for the Lord.

Proverbs 3:5-6

Trust in the Lord with all your heart; do not depend on your own understanding. Seek his will in all you do, and he will show you which path to take.

Psalm 147:3

He heals the brokenhearted and bandages their wounds.

1 Peter 5:8-10

Stay alert! Watch out for your great enemy, the devil. He prowls around like a roaring lion, looking for someone to devour. Stand firm against him, and be strong in your faith. Remember that your family of believers all over the world is going through the same kind of suffering you are. In his kindness God called you to share in his eternal glory by means of Christ Jesus. So after you have suffered a little while, he will restore, support, and strengthen you, and he will place you on a firm foundation.

Invisible Wounds

Isaiah 26:3

You will keep in perfect peace all who trust in you, all whose thoughts are fixed on you!

Deuteronomy 31:6

So be strong and courageous! Do not be afraid and do not panic before them. For the Lord your God will personally go ahead of you. He will neither fail you nor abandon you.

2 Corinthians 4:16-18

Therefore we do not lose heart. Though outwardly we are wasting away, yet inwardly we are being renewed day by day. For our light and momentary troubles are achieving for us an eternal glory that far outweighs them all. So we fix our eyes not on what is seen, but on what is unseen, since what is seen is temporary, but what is unseen is eternal.

Resources

I realize there are so, so many wonderful Christian resources out there. This list is relatively short for two reasons: 1.) I think too many options can be overwhelming, especially when you're already weary. 2.) I felt strongly that I should only list those resources that I had personal experience with and/or would specifically target some of the needs and struggles I've shared in this book. I will continue to add to this list on my website *(melindameans.com/resources)*.

I pray God will lead you to the exact resources that He wants to use in your life, whether they are included on this list or not.

Books

Lindsey Bell, *Unbeaten: How Biblical Heroes Rose Above Their Pain…And You Can Too.* [Kansas, CrossRiver Media Group, 2016]

L.B. Cowman and James Reimann, *Streams in the Desert: 365 Daily Devotional Readings* [Michigan, Zondervan, 1997]

Nancy Leigh DeMoss, *Lies Women Believe: And The Truth That Sets Them Free* [Illinois, Moody, 2002]

Suzanne Eller, *The Unburdened Heart: Finding the Freedom of Forgiveness* [Michigan, Revell, 2013]

Suzanne Eller, *The Mended Heart: God's Healing for Your Broken Places* [Michigan, Revell, 2014]

Jennifer Dukes Lee, *Love Idol: Letting Go of Your Need for Approval and Seeing Yourself through God's Eyes* [Illinois, Tyndale Momentum, 2014]

Carey Scott, *Untangled: Let God Loosen the Knots of Insecurity in Your Life* [Michigan, Revell, 2015]

Joni Eareckson Tada, *Pearls of Great Price: 366 Daily Devotional Readings* [Michigan, Zondervan, 2006]

Joni Eareckson Tada, *A Place of Healing: Wrestling with the Mysteries of Suffering, Pain, and God's Sovereignty* [Colorado, David C. Cook, 2015]

Stacey Thacker and Brooke McGlothin, *Hope for the Weary Mom: Let God Meet You In The Mess* [Oregon, Harvest House, 2015]

Websites

American Association for Christian Counselors, *aacc.net*

Lindsey Bell, *lindseymbell.com*

Rachel Britz, *rachelbritz.com*

Joni Eareckson, *joniandfriends.org*

Suzanne Eller, *tsuzanneeller.com*

Not Alone, *specialneedsparenting.net*

(in)courage, *incourage.me*

Carey Scott, *careyscotttalks.com*

Laurie Wallin, *lauriewallin.com*

Bible Studies

Jennie Allen, *Stuck: The Places We Get Stuck and the God Who Sets Us Free* [Tennessee, Thomas Nelson, 2011]

Wendy Blight, *I Know His Name: Discovering Power in the Names of God* (InScribed Collection) [Tennessee, Thomas Nelson, 2016]

Jessica LaGrone, *Namesake: Women's Bible Study Participant Book: When God Rewrites Your Story* [Tennessee, Abingdon Press, 2013]

Beth Moore, *Breaking Free (Bible Study Book): The Journey, The Stories*, Workbook Updated ed. [Tennessee, Lifeway Press, 2009]

Judy Rossi, *Enhancing Your Marriage: A Woman's Bible Study* [Tennessee, AMG, 2005]

Angela Thomas, *Stronger - Bible Study Book: Finding Hope in Fragile Places* [Tennessee, Lifeway Press, 2013]

Sheila Walsh, *The Storm Inside Study Guide: Trade The Chaos Of How You Feel For The Truth Of Who You Are* [Tennessee, Thomas Nelson, 2014]

If you were inspired and encouraged by this book, please consider sharing your positive experience in an Amazon review.

About the Author

Melinda Means is a soul in need of constant refreshment from the only Source who can quench our thirst. After years of chronic pain and bouts of questioning the love and goodness of a Savior who would allow it, she has learned to choose hope, freedom and Truth—moment by moment—despite her circumstances and emotions.

Melinda loves to speak and write for hurting women. She is Women's Director at her church and co-author of *Mothering From Scratch: Finding the Best Parenting Style for You and Your Family* (Bethany House, 2015). Her coaching business Revealed Coaching for Writers helps women bloggers, writers and speakers discover and passionately communicate their God-given messages and stories—the stories only they can tell. Her website is *melindameans.com*. She and her husband Mike have two children, teenage son Micah and a college-age daughter Molly.

Connect with Melinda

Visit my blog for a Survival Kit created just for you!

melindameans.com/survival-kit

Website and blog: *melindameans.com*

Email: *melindameansauthor@gmail.com*

Follow me on Pinterest:

https://www.pinterest.com/melindaauthor

Share Your Story as a guest writer on my blog!

melindameans.com/contact-us/share-your-story-guidelines

✿ ✿ ✿

Are you a writer or blogger looking for someone to help you tell your story?

Melinda is a professional writing coach.

Visit her website

melindameans.com/coaching/services-packages

to learn more about her coaching services.

Or email her at *melinda@revealedcoaching.com*.

Revealed
Coaching for Writers

Would you like Melinda to speak at an upcoming event for your church, group or organization?

Visit her website to learn more about her speaking topics *(http://melindameans.com/speaking/topics)*.

Other books by this author:

Melinda is also co-author of *Mothering From Scratch: Finding the Best Parenting Style For You and Your Family* (Bethany House, 2015).

It's available on Amazon and in most bookstores.

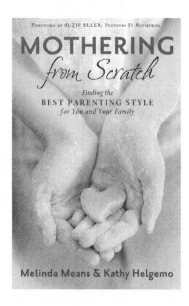

NOTES

Chapter 2

[1] Lee Strobel, "Why Does God Allow Tragedy and Suffering?" July 25, 2012, Bible Gateway, *https://www.biblegateway.com/blog/2012/07/why-does-god-allow-tragedy-and-suffering/*

[2] Tim Keller, *The Reason for God: Belief in an Age of Skepticism*, [New York, Penguin Books, 2009] p. 33

Chapter 3

[1] C. S. Lewis, *A Grief Observed* [New York, Bantam Books, 1961] p. 4

[2] Peter Scazzero, *Emotionally Healthy Spirituality*, [Michigan, Zondervan, 2006] p. 121

[3] Barnes Notes on the Bible, Genesis 32, *http://biblehub.com/commentaries/barnes/genesis/32.htm*

[4] John F. Walvoord and Roy B. Zuck (editors), *The Bible Knowledge Commentary*, Old Testament [Illinois, Victor Books a Division of Scripture Press Publications, Inc., 1985] p. 81

Chapter 4

[1] Sheila Walsh, *The Storm Inside Study Guide*, [Tennessee, Nelson Books, an imprint of Thomas Nelson, 2014] p. 48

Chapter 5

[1] Dr. Benjamin T. Mast, *Second Forgetting*, [Michigan, Zondervan, 2014] pgs. 84-85

[2] Alan Redpath, *Blessings out of Buffetings: Studies in Second Corinthians*, [Michigan, Fleming H Revell Company, 1993] p. 214

[3] Donald Grey Barnhouse, *Genesis: A Devotional Exposition* [Michigan, Zondervan, 1984], p.127

Chapter 7

[1] John F. Walvoord and Roy B. Zuck (editors), *The Bible Knowledge Commentary*, New Testament edition [Illinois, Victor Books a Division of Scripture Press Publications, Inc., 1983] p. 609

[2] Joe Bayly, *The View from a Hearse*, [Indiana, Warhorn Publishing, 2014] Kindle edition, Location 495

Made in the USA
Columbia, SC
23 November 2020

25308740R00090